# Picasso's World of Children

*Overleaf*
*The Artists*
*1905    Gouache    35½ × 20¾"*
*Staatsgalerie, Stuttgart*

# Picasso's World of Children

*by Helen Kay*

WITH AN INTRODUCTION BY DANIEL-HENRY KAHNWEILER

*A Chanticleer Press Edition*

DOUBLEDAY & CO. INC., GARDEN CITY, NEW YORK

*Pour ma famille*

*Reproductions by permission of French Reproduction Rights, Inc.*

*Edited, designed and produced by Chanticleer Press, Inc., New York*

*Printed in Italy*

*Published by Doubleday & Company, Inc.*

*A Windfall Book*

# Contents

# *Preface*

The combined age of the men who made this book possible was 239 years. They were three of the youngest people in the world—all about eighty years young. Each was still active in his field, receptive to ideas, still feverishly at work. I did not know them, nor they me; I had no recommendations, other than a few children's books to show, an explanation of what these pictures meant to me, and a dummy of some pictures. Most still had to be found and collected. I tried to frame the book in words. I tried to point out how many aspects of childhood Picasso had painted; how much of a traveler he was into its land.

When I explained the book to the poet Jaime Sabartès, eighty-one, Picasso's friend, biographer, secretary, he answered in his dour and gently pessimistic way: "Perhaps, because Picasso painted so much of everything, he painted much of children, too."

Four times I visited Sabartès at 7 rue des Grands-Augustins, "his empire for an hour a day," in Picasso's deserted Paris studio where the *Guernica* was painted. Daily, he climbed the four flights of stairs to the top floor to conduct business. I must have persuaded this man whom Picasso called "live coal of friendship / the clock that always strikes the hour…" for he helped obtain the permissions.

Daniel-Henry Kahnweiler, publisher and art authority, that launcher of new writers, aged seventy-seven, old friend and associate of Picasso, saw what I meant immediately, and his rosy face and sparkling blue eyes shone: "You are the first to see this book. You are to be congratulated." Thoughtfully, he added: "But you must include a dead child."

At Mougins, at *domaine de Notre-Dame-de-Vie,* where Picasso lived, two live coals for eyes looked through the "maquette" from the mountain of his eighty-one years and said: "When it is finished it will be a beautiful book."

# Introduction

BY DANIEL-HENRY KAHNWEILER

Nothing is further removed from an "abstract painting," one that signifies nothing, than a painting by Pablo Picasso. This is because nothing that is human is alien to him, nothing that constitutes man's universe: not animals, or plants, or objects. In the center of this world is mán himself.

You may remember, perhaps, a folk print of long ago entitled: "The Ages of Man." On one side was the child, the adolescent, the adult, climbing the steps; man in his full maturity stood at the top; then, starting on the other side, the descent ended with the old man dragging himself toward the grave. It would be possible to make many compositions of "the ages of man" with Picasso's work. He painted people of all ages: men, women, children. It is curious to note that in his first paintings (which date from 1895) one finds many old men. The child that he was must have been sensitive to the picturesque quality of these hairy, bearded beggars.

Nevertheless, if one wanted to establish some sort of statistics of Picasso's later subjects, it is quite certain that children would figure importantly. There is no esthetic reason for this. He has painted, drawn, etched, sculptured many children because he adores children, especially young ones. I have seen him affectionate at all times with the children about him. I remember him around 1908, kissing with tender sweetness the little hand of a baby, a child of friends. He painted or drew many of these children. Even more so did he cherish and sketch his own children: Paulo, Maya, Claude, Paloma. He made innumerable portraits of them. He depicted them nude, or dressed in masquerade. Those characterizations, needless to say, are in his "style" at the moment of their creation. It is significant that one, and only one, period would have

8

no portraits—not of a child, or of an adult, for that matter—the period of Cubism evolving from the analytical to the synthetic phase, that is, in the years 1911 to 1914. His preoccupation with grammar and syntax, so to say, kept him at this time from "individualizing" his figures, from doing "portraits."

The children painted or drawn by Picasso are of all ages. One can see them at every moment of their young lives. There are babies in the cradle, in their mother's arms, children playing, Paulo riding a donkey, Maya with a little boat, Claude and Paloma with a little toy train. There are children sick in bed. And then there are the dead children, victims of wars.

One must always remember that no art is more autobiographical than Picasso's. It is a perpetual confession. Such an art is more true, more sincere than any other that could be conceived. It is not only the esthetic emotions of the artist that he allows us to share with him, but also his joys and sorrows. If one stops to ponder this, one will realize that such an art that unveils the very life of its author is now appearing more and more often in literature, too. In *Remembrance of Things Past* Proust was still compelled to camouflage the story of his life as a novel. Today the best among the poets reveal their life story without disguise.

What then is esthetic enjoyment, the sensation of overwhelming happiness that we feel in front of works of art, whatever they are? Truly, it is our communion with the artist whose emotion—love, joy, or sadness—we share. People have often misunderstood what the Impressionists were fighting when they thundered against "anecdotal" art. They did not mean at all to deny an emotional content to their work; on the contrary, they meant to convey the sensations they experienced before a landscape they loved. They wanted to avoid disguising in Greco-Roman rags their love of a world they had just discovered. The Cubists cherished the simple objects that had been disdained before. Never has true painting been a purely technical exercise or pointless mural decoration. It has been a testimony of love.

What is it thus that makes us value so the last paintings of Rembrandt? Of course, *Caravaggisme* achieves a magical light and color there. But there is more: nothing is more human than these paintings. In them the lonely old man expresses his tender love for young Hendrikje Stoffels; his pity before the ravages of age deforming the feminine body in his Bathsheba, his painful resignation in his self-portraits. We are moved, we feel close to this man. The work of Pablo Picasso moves us just as Rembrandt's does. In Picasso's work, however, resignation is as yet absent. Certainly, in the drawings of the series, "The Painter and His Model," the ugliness of the old painter is in marked contrast to the radiant beauty of the young women, but Picasso always dresses up this old artist with a beard, never makes him a true self-portrait. He is not resigned to being this old painter; he revolts against disfiguring old age, does not accept it.

We, nevertheless, participate in his whole life, his joys and sorrows. His work, like that of Rembrandt, like the work of all great artists, resembles that gigantic coffin of which Heinrich Heine speaks in the last verse to his last poem:

*You know what makes my coffin*
*So large, so hard to bear?*
*I've laid my love within it,*
*And my too-heavy care.*

As for this book that assembles the pictures of children created by Pablo Picasso, it is a hymn to young life. Certainly grief enters it, with mourning before the dead children, victims of ghastly hangmen; but hope survives and life is born anew in spite of insatiable death.

This exultant *ronde des enfants* is its unimpeachable testimony.

# I      *A Catalogue of Childhood*

Pablo Picasso looked up from his sketchbook at his children dancing, and then drew a *ronde des enfants*. His children, playing, proclaimed the right of all children to play. He stamped the personal with the universal and so brought forth a symbol of enduring life. Because of that innate understanding of beginnings which is rooted in himself, he captured the sights and sounds and smells of childhood.

The man who has been called "an inventive spirit in continuous eruption" is, like William Blake, a "master of contraries." He, too, can sing a song of innocence; he, too, can fathom hell. Blake could ask: "Little Lamb, who made thee?" (1789), and Picasso could draw *Paulo with a Lamb* (1923). They were both painter-poets, revolutionaries in their time. To Picasso all the arts are the same: "You can write a picture in words, just as you can paint sensations in a poem," and he picked up his stylus and etched in acid a poem-picture of his young son Claude and, using words, he wrote a picture-poem: "the child of 1 and the other."

Picasso's paintings of children come during two great spans of time: those belonging to his early years until he was about twenty-five, and those painted during his proud, boastful fatherhood and full maturity—from forty to seventy.

During the Blue Period and the Rose Period, he touched delicately, tenderly, and always evocatively the most poignant aspects of childhood. At other times he was only looking at children out of the corner of his eye. Then, while he was painting *Les Demoiselles d'Avignon* (1907), and fathering Cubism, he became so preoccupied with purely formal problems that he had no time for even this glance—here pictures of children occur very rarely. But once more, from 1921 to 1953, Picasso looked at children from all conceivable angles. His models were his own—and so twice fashioned.

These two hundred picture documents measured against the total mass of his work are but a moment in the full hour of his creativity. Yet, like the small candle (lighted as much by technical as by human considerations) that turned blue into a period, these two hundred pictures shed light—they illumine the human base of Picasso's work.

In the beginning, his subjects were relatives, children of friends and of his imagination. As early as 1896, when he was fifteen, Picasso introduced an infant in arms into the picture called *Science and Charity*. Here, his father was the model for the doctor. As two of his aunts were nuns, one of them might well have been the Sister of Charity holding the baby. His sister Lola and his aunt Pepa posed for him, as did an old servant of his Uncle Salvador, the doctor who had brought him into the world. Later, Picasso drew and painted chiefly from memory. He often found his subjects in the streets of Barcelona and Paris. His *Little Girl, Rear View* (1899), and signed PRP (Pablo Ruiz Picasso), appeared unrehearsed before him. And so did a mother, dragging her little ones with her on her busy round: *The Mother* (1901). There, too, he found poor street urchins—*Three Children* (1903)—as free gifts to his memory.

Children wander in and out of the Blue and Rose Periods. The Blue Period child is symbolic: a telling reminder of Picasso's religious background. Even a bowl of soup is carried as though it were a ritual vessel: *La Soupe* (1902). The *Family Supper* (1903), with both parents attendant on the child, is a holy supper: *La Famille au Souper*. So is the relationship of *Mother and Child* (1901), where the flowing mantle gives comfort emotionally, and artistically it gives a sculptured quality to their prayerful attitudes. In the Blue Period, the unity of mother and child is rarely disturbed.

The Circus Period bridges the Blue and the Rose. Much of the religious feeling characteristic of the Blue has vanished. The child, not yet wholly independent, becomes the searcher as he grows up—an uncommitted observer of the life around him. Standing dead center in the large *Saltimbanques* (1905) he does not know where his path leads: to his mother (who seems absorbed in her own problems) or to his comrades. This ambivalence runs through the pictures of these early years. In the *Artists*

12

*Claude, 1949*
*Detail from "Poèmes et Lithographies"*
*Galerie Louise Leiris, Paris*

(1905), the boy sits with his mother, misery shared, yet each unable to comfort the other, each looking his separate way, together yet alone... the food uneaten. In *Death of Harlequin* (1905), the boy has already been warned of the loneliness of life.

These early works of the "Picasso-Before-Picasso" years remain constants in an art world of sudden and almost frenetic changes in taste. They touch the heart and move deeply. The best of these early canvases are perfect of their sort, and it scarcely matters that Picasso's most important work came later. Looking upon these masterpieces of unchanging beauty, we feel certain they must have come effortlessly, and without calculation, from the painter's brush. Yet, there were always sketches behind the pictures, innumerable sketches and studies. Sometimes they preceded the pictures, sometimes they were sketched on canvas, and sometimes they were even dashed off after the painting was finished—a quick curtain call of Picasso's memory.

Despite these early masterpieces, to those who think only of Picasso as a discoverer and the master experimentalist of the twentieth century, he was born artistically about 1906, came of age with *Les Demoiselles d'Avignon* (1907), spurred a world revolution with Cubism, and thereafter became front-page news with every new style that he created. During the fourteen or fifteen years from 1907 to 1921, Picasso had little time to converse on childhood, either in pictures or words.

Then came the birth of a son—Paulo, his first child, in 1921. Once again the theme of maternity—the closeness of mother and child occurs. Here the giant mothers of Picasso's Neoclassic Period symbolize his extravagant joy in his parenthood.

The birth of a son meant so much to Picasso that he never sold a picture of Paulo alone, though two representations of the child with his mother Olga were sold in later years. He has always hated to sell pictures that he loves for personal reasons. Thus began his personal collection, the most intimate part of which Picasso himself called the "Family Gallery." Here he keeps the pictures of his children.

The multiple representations of Paulo, of Maya, of Claude, of Paloma, produce a composite portrait, utterly individual, for each of these children.

These pictures Picasso painted for his own pleasure. In their totality, they reflect the whole gamut of the child's inner and outer life: the child's needs and what he feeds on; how he grows; his toys—which are equally his work; his sense of make-believe; his sense of wonder; his sorrows and his joys. Picasso captured all that a child is—all the child's awkwardness and grace. Many artists have painted more children, but no one has equaled Picasso in discovering the poetry of a child's world.

It follows, then, that Picasso has painted children only as a labor of love. The commissioned works can be counted on the fingers of one hand: the Soler children (1903), Allan Stein (1906), the wife and children of the art dealer Paul Rosenberg (1918). He painted them to pay for vests, miscellaneous favors—and friendship.

Picasso's art is a never-ending series of monologues on the human condition. His representations of children explore the sources of the human condition—the childhood of man. His cycle of childhood, sketched and etched, drawn, painted, molded and shaped, lithographed, chalked, fired, and carved over a long lifetime, scampers, bounds, and dances through the vast theater of his creative achievement. If the curtain falls briefly on a scene, the poignancy and nostalgic persistence of that scene endures

*Little Girl with Hat*
*1901    Oil    29½ × 20"*
*Fogg Art Museum, Harvard University*
*Maurice Wertheim Collection*

14

and is picked up again in still another scene or act of this drama of life. For it is the drama of life that Picasso loves, and here are its very roots.

Picasso is the painter of the child's more important status in the world. He has shown that the artist, like society itself, must make countless voyages of discovery into the realm of childhood. Two hundred years ago a child was considered a plaything, a moppet, even a dwarfed adult. Children were thought of as little men and little women, and were so treated. Only after Rousseau did society begin to look at children as children—with their own needs, rights, and dignity. The poets, more intuitive and sympathetic than most, came first in seeing the child vividly and whole: "The child is father of the man." The child's sense of wonder, carried into adulthood, plays a large role in the artist's creative magic.

Pablo Picasso, as he turned his eye and his brush on childhood's estate, is a poet. He feels a kinship with both Rousseaus—the philosopher Jean-Jacques and the painter Henri (the *douanier*). The philosopher taught man to think of the primitive within him, and the primitive painter saw the world mirrored in the pond of his childhood. The young Picasso sought out and honored the *douanier,* when all Paris laughed at him.

Picasso has said: "The first of the *douanier*'s work that I had the opportunity of acquiring [for five francs, as usable canvas] took hold of me with the force of obsession." Today Picasso has his own private collection of Rousseau's paintings.

Since Picasso was a child prodigy and was carefully taught in the academic manner, he never drew—like Rousseau—in a childlike way; he had to learn that later from his own children. He delighted in getting down on his hands and knees and drawing as the children did. In learning how to sketch a child's world through their eyes, he may have become the most sophisticated primitive that ever was.

How does the child see?

Gertrude Stein in *Picasso* (1938) said it well—and it scarcely matters that she was simultaneously explaining the logic of Cubism:

> *A child sees the face of its mother, it sees it in a completely different way than other people see it. I am not speaking of the spirit of the mother, but of the features*

16

*of the whole face, the child sees it from very near, it is a large face for the age of a*
*small one, it is certain the child for a little while only sees a part of the face of its*
*mother. It knows one feature and not another, one side and not the other, and in*
*his way Picasso knows faces as a child knows them and the head and the body.*

Picasso sees as the child sees, and he sees as the mother sees, for he is a master of simultaneous vision. He sees and dissects the simple and the complex, showing them at one and the same time. This simultaneity of sensory response, which often shapes his vision, may be painful, since the pictorial evidence betrays the agony of creation.

Here is the painter-poet talking, paraphrased somewhat: he hears the cries of children and at the same time hears all cries—of beds, chairs, birds, stones, odors, smoke even. That was Spain in 1937. When he looked at his wife he saw every part of her, and dug beneath the sinews, the blood, the guts, and those intimate parts which the Princess Katharine of France, in Shakespeare's *Henry V,* blushed to name before the *"seigneurs de France";* all these he named—even the "belly full of bones" that was to be his child: *Paloma* (1949). Some of this he said, and some he painted.

Picasso's output is prodigious. In all his eighty years, there was only a one-year period when he ceased working. In the five years between 1900 and 1905, he painted two hundred pictures, the equivalent of a lifetime of work for some artists.

In 1901, he was turning out two or three pictures a day. Christian Zervos catalogued, through 1944, more than seven thousand separate works in thirteen large volumes: paintings, drawings, pieces of sculpture. Twenty years later, Picasso was still producing in various media, always at a feverish pace: discarding old forms, inventing new ones, and as late as 1963 humorously discussing a machine to speed up the application of color so that the artist could paint as rapidly as he saw.

During Picasso's first winter in Paris, he ran out of canvas, paper, and board. He looked about the studio for old pictures to resurface. Backs were best—they provided a clean start. And so the little girl with the long honey-colored hair and the big hat was reversed, and the great green *Woman with a Chignon* (1901) was painted on the clean surface. This double picture, belonging to Mrs. Maurice Wertheim of New

York, has the *Little Girl with the Hat* (1901) facing the wall. Like a naughty child who has been stood in the corner until she behaves, the *Little Girl with a Hat* must be picked up and turned around gently to be seen. "I do not know who the child is, but I know that Picasso hates her," Mrs. Wertheim said.

*Three Children* (1903), forlorn and pensive beggars, were also relegated to the blank wall when Picasso made a watercolor of the *Brooding Woman* (1904).

One child, however, triumphed over an adult. With bold splashes of color Picasso painted out the mature face and figure of a standing woman. Then he painted the

*Blind Minotaur, Number 1*
*1934    Etching    10 × 13 ¾"*

tender *Child with Dove* (1901). Lady Aberconway, the present owner, felt two pairs of eyes looking down on her as she worked at her desk, and when the painting was leaving her study for the Picasso Exhibition at the Tate Gallery in 1960, she asked the Courtauld Institute to x-ray it. The secret behind the *Child with Dove* was revealed more than half a century after it was painted. Art historians also suspect that *La Soupe* (1902) was painted over another picture, though it has not as yet been x-rayed.

*Child with Dove* is one of the tenderest of Picasso's paintings of children. Yet, tender though it is, poetically so, it is also decisive. There is not a falsely sentimental note about it. Whatever the style he elects to use, he always sees, piercingly. His later picture documents of the child's world seek out the bone and the marrow—and the brattishness, too. A clumsy line, deliberately chosen, delineates the awkwardness of growing up. Picasso points a loving finger at clumsy spontaneity. He adores the natural clown. This unsentimental record, however, does not avoid the round cheek or the innocent eye. They are there, but often seen profile and front face together, like a blurred movie photograph, as if the child cannot sit still long enough to pose.

Absorbed in a most sophisticated theme—Manet's *Déjeuner sur l'herbe,* Picasso made his *Les Déjeuners* (1961) entirely his own by placing a child with his playthings in the foreground of the bathers. The child reaches out to taste and conquer life.

As in *Les Déjeuners,* the child is enlisted as a multiple symbol, and as a symbol he weaves in and out of Picasso's work.

A little girl with flowers and later a pigeon leads the beast in *The Blind Minotaur* (1934) like a domesticated animal. In the *Minotauramachy* (1935), she holds a lighted lamp. In his mural, *Peace,* a small boy plows the field with Pegasus, the horse of horses; and childish mischief, unimpressed by tradition, makes a happy world (1952). Here, too, he honored the innate wisdom of childhood by placing a pet owl, Athena fashion, on a small boy's head. Claude was then five years old. Paloma was three.

Looking throughout the years at children in all their variety... looking with his sophisticated, primitive eye, Picasso echoes Blake: "The child's toys and the old man's reasons / Are the fruit of the two seasons."

*Facing page*
*Little Girl, Rear View*
*1899    Watercolor    6½ × 3½"*
*Dr. and Mrs. Andrew M. Linz, New York*

*The Destitute's Meal*
*1903    Watercolor    11 × 14"*

# 2

# *Who Are These Children?*

PICASSO was his mother's name. His father was Don José Ruiz. Pablo Picasso was the name he finally chose for himself from a long necklace of names. As the first-born son of Don José and Donna María he was baptized: Pablo in honor of an uncle, a canon of the Cathedral of Málaga; Diego for his grandfather on his father's side; José for his father, ninth child of Diego and brother of the uncle Pablo; Francisco de Paula for his maternal grandfather; Juan Nepomuceno, the Spanish form for the national saint of Bohemia, Jon of Nepomuk, and also the first names of his godfather and cousin Blasco y Barrosa; María de los Remedios, a particular title of the Virgin Mary; Cipriano de la Santisima Trinidad, for a saint especially venerated in Andalusia. His parents were Andalusians: for them "a rosary of names" was customary.

He might have used both his father's and his mother's names, Ruiz y Picasso, as most Spaniards do, and for a time he did. Afterward he shortened it to the initials PRP. Then he adopted his mother's name and signed it with his father's brush. It was less plain than *Ruiz,* meaning rice, and the relative unusualness of the name Picasso seemed, to his admiring comrades, to single him out for fame.

His father was an art teacher, a pigeon fancier, a bullfight *aficionado*. Pablo learned all he could teach him: he went to the bullfights with him; he held his cane, his hat, his hand, his arm, his brushes, a pigeon, as they walked to school. He took something of his father's into class. He needed some assurance that his father would return for him and take him from the hated place called school. Formal learning came hard. He could not add, he could not write, he could not read, but he could draw. For years his mother prized a table, completely covered with his sketches.

*Three Children*
*1903   Watercolor   14½ × 10⅝"*
*Museum of Modern Art, New York*
*Gift of Mr. and Mrs. Werner E. Josten*

Don José was so worried by his son's seeming dullness that he arranged for a friend to give the boy the entrance examination. Pablo's answers were: "But I do not know." He could not tell his examiner that he only wanted to draw all the time.

Picasso related to his biographer and friend Roland Penrose how the kindly teacher resolved the dilemma. Instead of asking questions, he wrote numbers on the blackboard, and Picasso copied them. He copied exactly. To Picasso, these numbers were pictures. "I shall copy the little pigeon," he said to himself. "The eye of a pigeon is round like a zero... there are two eyes and two wings.... The two legs placed on the table underline it, and below that there is the total."

"You see, you did know," the examiner said. "The rest will come later." So Picasso passed.

A Sunday without a bullfight was a disastrous day... a colorless eternity, occasionally lighted by the yellow from a sticky taffy. He could build castles in the clouds on the jagged contours his teeth had cut; then he could see through the transparency, licked thin as isinglass. The memory of color was so vivid that in his maturity Picasso could recall it in detail to Jaime Sabartès.

Above all, he remembered his father always painting pigeons. Don José's rooms were full of pigeons, either free or in coops for the night. "Lots of pigeons on their perches. Imagine a cage with hundreds of pigeons in it... with thousands of pigeons— thousands and millions...." The pigeon and the child became partners. Children and pigeons represented two main themes of his life and were united in one picture painted in Paris in 1901, *Child with Dove*—symbols that were to run through his life again and again.

The picture is reminiscent of Goya's Don Manuel Osorio Manrique de Zuñiga, Lord of Gines, an important child. Goya told about the little lord with the magpie, tame, but on a string; his birds are caged, his cats are watchful, and the child looks frightened. Picasso, too, was more interested in telling about his child than in merely portraying him. Gently holding the free bird to its breast, the child stirs warmth and tenderness; yet the boldness of the outline and the brushwork keeps the picture from

*Christening Card of Child of Pere Romeu*
*1902    Ink sketch*

being maudlin, and gives it vigor. This is one of Picasso's early surprises. As heavily outlined as a Van Gogh, it is not a Spanish picture.

*Child with Dove* was painted over a picture of a standing woman. Thick applications of color in the background altogether wiped out the mature face and figure. At the child's feet is a poignant symbol: this variegated ball holds the worldly experiences the child must face.

Who were the children whom Picasso was painting in these early days? Picasso's answer was: "But they are no one. I made them up."

Childhood is a very short-lived state—yet it lives with us always. The outer child disappears; lost in a few years, but within the adults we become, the small child continues to inhabit our house and haunt us all our lives.

There are several elements that brought these partly real, partly imaginary children into being. First of all, he was both nurtured and harassed by his own nostalgic feeling as an indulged first-born son. Perhaps it was the wish for children that the reluctantly maturing youth could not fulfill until half his life was gone: his first child was born

*Portrait of a Child*
*1904    Pen drawing*

when he was forty, his last daughter when he was sixty-seven. Add to these the remembrance of his two small sisters: Lola, who often posed for him as a child, and—even more haunting in bringing image to life—Conchita, who was just a memory, the fair-haired small sister who had died of diphtheria at seven.

Most of Picasso's pictures of children show the small ones. They stop abruptly, anywhere from six to eight years old. It was the period of wonderment that he was most bemused with—he loved the beginners. At eighty plus, he himself still has that air of wonder—a controlled innocence.

"Listen to your childhood, to the hour that white in the blue memory borders white..." he can say; and he goes back in time himself. He was recognized as a prodigy from the age of seven. His fingers were so facile and his eyes so exact that he could obey the multiple demands of his young sisters and cousins.

"Make me a horse!" ordered Cousin María. "No, a pigeon!" from Concha. "But I want a doll!" pleaded his sister Lola. There were so many small girls to please and amuse. He would start his drawings ever in a new place: the foot or the hand, the

26

ear or the belly of the horse, the red round eye of a pigeon or its tail, and like magic the image would appear on paper or in the sand, where he drew it with a stick, or in his hand as a cut-out with a scissors. "I drew long before I could speak," Picasso has said, "but I never drew like a child."

At fourteen Picasso was admitted to the advanced class at La Lonja, the Barcelona art school after completing in a single day the work for which a month was normally allowed. He was already known as *"el pintor."* At sixteen, he demonstrated the same speed and skill before the examiners of the Royal Academy of San Fernando, in Madrid. But the academic road was too routine, and he was saved from continuing on it by scarlet fever, which sent him into the countryside to convalesce. The wretchedness of life among the poor peasants was imprinted on his mind, and his empathy illuminated his canvases.

Picasso, when scarcely more than a boy, turned often to the theme of mothers and their children. A child with a small doll, a barefoot boy, a sick infant with a feverish face, a newborn baby being nursed, a mother stopping work to kiss her little girl, a mother and her baby boy—these subjects haunted him. But he sent them out nameless. They were no one. The picture told all. Over and over when asked to title a canvas or name it, Picasso would ask a dealer: "What for?" and then say the first thing that came into his head. Mostly the dealers named them. He was too busy painting.

Picasso considers the way art dealers, critics, and collectors christen pictures a mania. Jaime Sabartès said: "Some like to give titles; others to change them. As for him, he never gives any to his works."

That is how some of his pictures came to acquire as long a string of names as his own. The child scraping the last contents of a pudding bowl is variously called *Greedy Child,* or *La Petite Gourmande,* or *Le Gourmand* (as Zervos calls it), since despite the long hair and dress, no one knows whether the child is a boy or a girl; all small children at the turn of the century wore the same kind of clothes. This painting with its impressions of Gauguin, strong and sweet, has also been called *Sweet Tooth.* The National Gallery of Art in Washington, D.C., prefers *The Gourmet* (1901), by which name it has been known for over thirty of the sixty-odd years of its existence.

Although Picasso called them "children of the imagination"—and used no professional models, he did in fact paint pictures of children so real that one could smell the bread and butter they had just been eating. To them names can be given. For example, there was an early one of his small sister Lola, in a nightgown and barefoot, holding a large doll in her lap (1896), a gift from her parents to offset jealousy. When the artist was given a roll of canvas, the model was given a doll.

In later years when his friends of the Four Cats, that collection of young and rebellious Catalan poets and artists, had children, he honored those occasions.

For Pere Romeu and his English Corinne, the hosts of the Four Cats, he made a christening card on the birth of a boy, Pere Romeu Jauregui, on May 12, 1902. The painter Ricardo Canals' son Octavio was sketched as a hungry waif (1904), with great greedy eyes, staring at a well-laid table. But then they were all hungry. Picasso gave the tailor Soler, whom they all called "Patches," many paintings in payment for the proper, tightly fitting trousers and vests he liked to wear at the time. Most memorable was a family portrait, *The Soler Family Picnic* (1903), with the solemn faces of the four Soler children shining from a blue background. The blue was reapplied in later years to cover the horror of a grotto put in by an enthusiast for literalism. Picasso, as he was hurriedly leaving for Paris, had asked a friend to full in the background.

In tragic days a Spanish Republican exile brought to the Goya museum at Castres the graphite of a child that Picasso had made in 1903, and sold it for a "little something," because he was "in need at the time." Ultimately Picasso recognized his work; he signed and authenticated it, but he did not remember the child.

Picasso always found real children to paint or draw or become friends with, whatever his age. Among them were the three little children of the artist Van Dongen, all girls, who lived close to Picasso in Montmartre. In their company he spent hours, especially enjoying the drollness of the youngest, who called him "Tablo."

Below his window he watched the concierge's little daughter play hopscotch and jump rope, a framed picture "so sweet" that he hoped she would never grow up.

*Child with Dove*
*1901    Oil    28¾ × 21¼"*
*Lady Aberconway, London*

*Soler Family Picnic*
*1903    Oil    60 × 80″*
*Musée des Beaux-Arts, Liège*

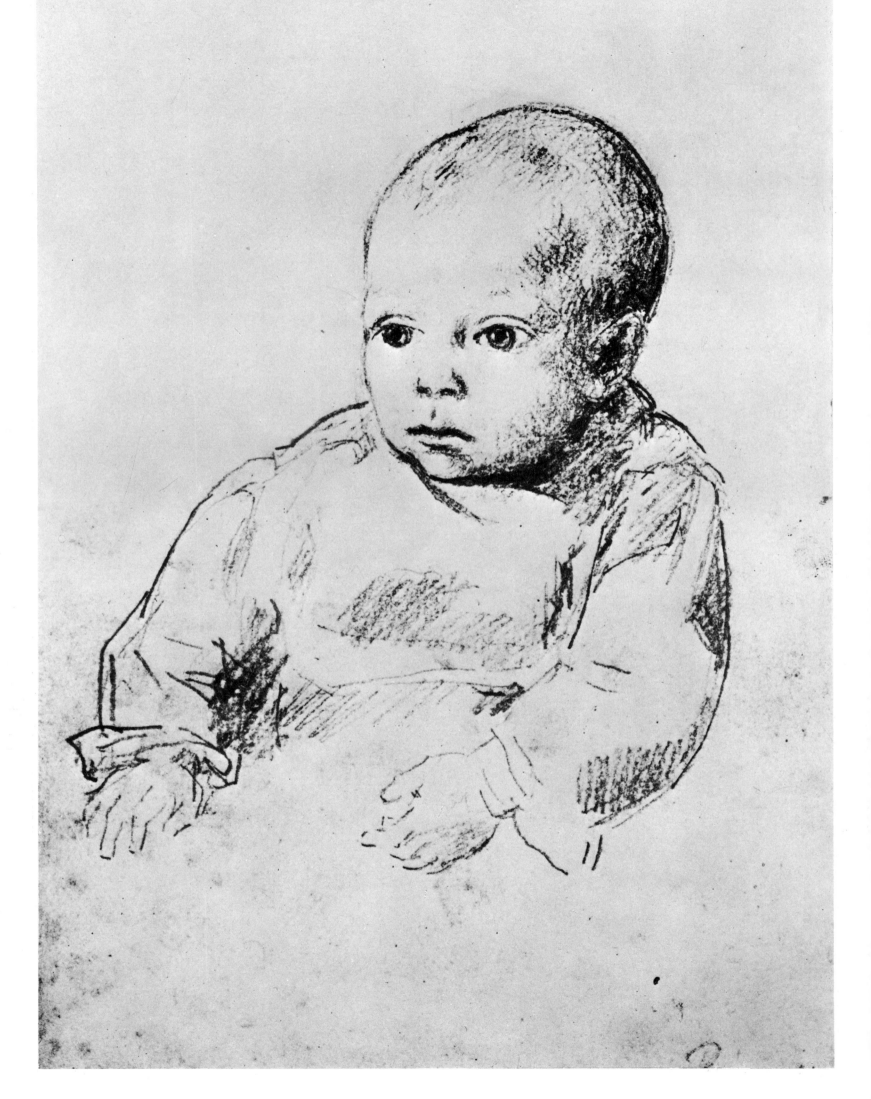

# 3

# *Yo El Rey*

Three times he wrote *Yo el Rey*—"I am the king"—over a self-portrait on the eve of his first trip to Paris in the last month of his eighteenth year. He had foretold the legend; he now had to live it. In paying for the trip, his parents had left themselves only a few pesetas to finish out the whole month. But Picasso did not know that.

An advance party from the Four Cats had preceded him to Paris; they found him a studio previously used by Isidro Nonell, another artist from the same band of Catalans who wandered back and forth across the Pyrenees from Barcelona, that attic window from the roof of Spain onto France and the rest of Europe.

Picasso met with success at once. He sold three drawings of bullfights to Berthe Weill for one hundred francs and acquired a patron, Pedro Mañach, an industrialist from Barcelona with a taste for collecting. He offered Picasso one hundred and fifty francs a month for his whole output. It was a start.

Since Picasso had promised his mother to be home by Christmas, he headed south again for Barcelona, returning "somewhat faded by the intemperate climate of Montmartre." He had been to Paris and acquired a new name, "Little Goya," which the seer of their little band, Miguel Utrillo, had given him after seeing Picasso's work at the Four Cats. Now he was a professional, no longer merely a talented student.

His friends had decided that it was time for an exhibition, and led by Jaime Sabartès, they had tacked unframed Picasso pastels directly onto the bare walls until there was no room to see whether there was paint or wallpaper beneath and the pictures spilled out of the room and down the hallway. The show attracted very little attention. Eventually Utrillo's review appeared in *Pel y ploma* and took note of

*The Gourmet*
*1901    Oil    36×27"*
*National Gallery of Art, Washington, D.C.*
*Chester Dale Collection*

Picasso's characteristics. "The art of Picasso is very young: the child of his observing spirit which does not pardon the weaknesses of the youth of our time and reveals even the beauty of the horrible, which he notes with the sobriety of one who draws because he sees and not because he can draw a nose from memory."

In Barcelona, Picasso soon received angry letters from Mañach urging him to return to Paris. The patron had nothing to show for his financial backing. However, when Picasso finally returned with his full folio, Mañach was so pleased that he let Picasso live in his own small suite and introduced him to Ambroise Vollard, the art dealer. Arrangements were then and there made for a first show at 6, rue Laffitte.

Picasso already had seventy-five pictures to exhibit, among them many of children. On June 24, 1901, he shared Vollard's gallery with a now wholly forgotten Basque painter named Francisco de Iturrino, almost twice Picasso's age. Iturrino's name was listed above Picasso's.

The fact that Picasso's pictures were "in the style" of Van Gogh, Daumier, Gauguin, and Toulouse-Lautrec attracted comment from the art critics, as did the extreme youth of the artist and the display of a virile talent. Heading his comment "The Spanish Invasion," Félicien Fagus, a critic for *La Revue Blanche,* wrote:

> *Picasso is a painter, absolutely and beautifully; his power of divining the substance of things should suffice to prove it.... Like all pure painters he adores color in itself, and to him each substance has its own color. Also he is in love with every subject, and to him everything is a subject ... there are discoveries: three little girls dancing, the practical green skirt over white underclothes which are so exactly that stiff boyish white of little girls' starched petticoats; the yellow and white of a woman's hat, etc.... It is evident that his passionate surge forward has not yet left him the leisure to forge for himself a personal style; his personality exists in this passion, this juvenile impetuous spontaneity.*

Félicien Fagus was able to acquire the painting of the dancing girls in 1903; he later sold it to the collector Pierre Lièvre in 1921. Even after Fagus' review appeared,

Picasso's pictures did not sell. However, he made a devoted and helpful friend—Max Jacob.

Jacob lived on small jobs—as a tutor to children, as a clerk—what he could get. At this time he was temporary secretary to the philanthropist-lawyer Henri Rollet, who organized an exhibition at the Petit Palais on the Champs-Elysées on the theme, "Childhood through the Ages." Rollet later became a judge of the children's courts, and Max Jacob became one of the great poets of France, but that day Jacob was attracted to Vollard's gallery because of the many paintings of children there. After he had seen them, he ran to find Pablo Picasso, the young painter, because he wished to be his friend. Thus began the long relationship between Picasso and the poets.

Through that long winter Picasso painted two or three canvases a day. Yet he grew more and more morose. In Mañach's tiny suite he complained to the ever-present band of invading Spaniards of the crowding and the small stipend. He began to resent his patron. Finally he packed up and went home. Back in Barcelona, he shared a corner of a studio among familiar surroundings, and painted. Meanwhile in Paris, Mañach was organizing another exhibition at Berthe Weill's gallery just down the street from Vollard on the rue Laffitte.

Thirty paintings and pastels, mostly from the previous year, were exhibited in this new show (April 1–15, 1902). Now the royal blue robe of one small child in a chair, *Baby in Blue* (1901), portended things to come. It was that exact color, declares Christian Zervos, "which Picasso utilizes from this time until the beginning of the Blue Period, from the end of 1901 to the spring of 1904."

Once again there was praise, but no one bought pictures. That third winter in Paris was a hard one.

Picasso sold only a single picture, *Mother and Child on the Shore* (1903), of a sturdy child striding purposefully beside a strong mother. He sold it for sixty francs. He had wanted two hundred. He no longer even had Mañach's allowance. Then Max Jacob had Picasso share a room with him. Since they had but a single bed, Picasso slept all

*Overleaf*
*Ronde des Enfants*
*Circa 1900    Oil    14¾ × 22¼"*
*M. and Mme Frédéric Schnerb, Paris*

day while Jacob worked, and then worked all night while Jacob slept—an arrangement that ended when Jacob lost his clerking job.

Before returning home for the last time (1903), Picasso—quite in the grimmest style of *La Bohème*—burned piles of drawings to keep warm. Altogether he went back and forth four times between Barcelona and Paris before settling down in the spring of 1904. Max Jacob named the new studio, the "Bateau Lavoir," laundry boat, since it so resembled the barges on the river where women washed their clothes. It was a festering old tenement on the rue Ravignon. Here, amid the shacks, sheds, and chimneypots that cluttered the hillside of Montmartre, in the very shadow of the Sacré-Cœur, Picasso was to live until fame caught up with him. Paris had finally become his home.

In these days and ever thereafter, Picasso adopted one animal after another until he had collected around him, rather like a pagan Saint Francis, a small zoo. He began modestly by gathering some needy neighborhood cats as well as a stray dog. In a drawer, he housed a tame white mouse with a tiny enough appetite; he had trained it to perform when he pulled open the drawer. Later, he added a turtle, a she-ape named Monina, two other dogs, and three cats. Frika, Picasso's dog of 1908, appears prominently in a group portrait by Marie Laurencin, including the poet Guillaume Apollinaire, Marie herself, Picasso, and Fernande Olivier.

Now in 1904, it was the tender way in which he held a kitten in his arms that brought Fernande Olivier into his life, though he continued to have difficulty feeding both human and animal friends. One of the cats helped to stave off their hunger, Fernande Olivier reported, by leaping into their room through a window—trailing a string of sausages.

*Barefoot Boys*
*1903    Pastel    14½ × 10½"*
*Thannhauser Foundation, New York*

Picasso.

*Facing page*
*The Mother*
*1901    Oil    29½ × 20"*
*City Art Museum of St.Louis*


*Child with Doll*
*1900    Oil    9⅝ × 13¼"*
*City Museum of Grenoble*

# 4

# *Why Blue?*

There had been blue pictures before the fall of 1901 and there were blue pictures after the spring of 1904, but they were not of that intense monochrome that characterizes the period called blue—the color that was the same royal blue as the robe of the *Baby in Blue* (1901), first known as *Child Seated in a Chair*.

Why did Picasso paint this way? There are many theories. Gertrude Stein, who knew him later, thought that something in Barcelona had stirred him. Afterward, Guillaume Apollinaire sang of this color: "Blue as the humid depths of an abyss and full of pity."

Picasso's famous blue is the blue of misery—the blue of cold fingers, chilblains, bloodless lips, and hunger. It was the blue of despair, of everlasting blue Sundays and Mondays, of the ambiguous blue note of jazz.

For Picasso, who has been called "the most human of humans," came to understand poverty through experience and compassion. He identified with the poorest, the most destitute, the most pitiful, with the bleakest aspect of life and with the "bluest of blue" in the human condition. He viewed all with "profound and frank stupefaction," and produced a series of memorable social studies.

As Picasso was a storyteller until he became a Cubist, his choice of this depressing blue tone accorded with his depressing subject matter.

Of course, there were those who explained his choice of blue in more practical terms. Some said that he could afford only a single tube of paint. He was poor, but he managed to find canvas, board, or—at worst—cardboard, and get enough paint for two or three pictures a day. If he had needed another tube, he would have found it.

*Baby in Blue*
*1901    Oil    25½ × 21¼"*
© *The Barnes Foundation, Merion, Pa.*

His palette was blue, but he mingled other colors, too—they hung on its edge and in the center was a mountain of white.

Others claim that he chose blue because he worked by night with only an oil lamp, and in the dark the world became blue. When the oil gave out, he used a candle, like another great night painter, Caravaggio, who sometimes had worked in a basement by candlelight. Some suggest that perhaps Picasso used blue because blue had a special luminosity by night.

Still others say that his obsession with blue was simply Picasso imitating Isidro Nonell, a member of the same little Spanish group, who also painted in monochrome. At one time Picasso used the same studio that Nonell had occupied when he had visited Paris. But Picasso was already painting his first blue pictures when Nonell was back in Barcelona. If he was echoing a monochromatic style, it was more likely that the French painter Eugène Carrière, a talented traditionalist who often used a gloomy gray palette, inspired him. He made a study of a Carrière mother and child, *The Sick Child* (1903), also known as *Mother and Child with Fichu,* which has remained in the Barcelona Museum of Modern Art. And once Picasso playfully signed Carrière's name to his own *Two Children* (1902) and sold it for a few pesetas, with his own name beneath.

Finally some say Picasso was so taken by the blue prints that photographers used as a cheaper substitute for other more costly negatives that he began to concentrate on blue. At one point he was reduced to blue ink alone, as in *Head of a Woman* (1903) and in *The Poor* (1904). Indeed, the more desperate the human condition, the more blue the painting.

Throughout Picasso's long career, he has always been interested, first of all, in those formal elements of his art which can be emphasized—if need be—without color or without an equal interest in color. Perhaps this best explains these monochromatic blues—this willingness to sacrifice color to design. It would not be too much to say that Picasso can be positively absentminded about color as he explores those elements which excite him most.

Anyhow, these answers must suffice for Picasso's trend toward blue. Add to them a self-consciousness inseparable from making so persistent a choice—a self-consciousness at once naive and sophisticated. So, we find Picasso choosing a new style in dress. The tight matador type of clothing of previous days, extravagant and costly now, was discarded. Picasso chose an appropriate uniform for these impoverished years— a blue overall and pullover such as Parisian plumbers wore, together with a short blue jacket. An affectation? No... he was poorer than a Paris plumber. Fernande Olivier in *Picasso and His Friends*, her filtered-through-time memories of those early years, wrote that the garments "acquired a delightful pastel shade from frequent washings."

He was young and proud and Spanish, and though Andalusian born, he had absorbed the independence and rebelliousness of the Basque character. He even found a Basque grandmother on his mother's side to boast about. Yet only a German word described his despair: *weltschmerz*.

He was not yet twenty when he began working in blue, utterly abandoning the varied subject matter of his teens and turning single-mindedly to the human figure, without, however, those bolder structural adventures which made him later the fore-most experimentalist in modern art.

Hope shone, in the blue, through the children. If there was a child in the picture, the child was a symbol of hope. Along with the children, spots of color frequently give a lift to these dejected pictures: the blind *Old Jew* (1903) has a bright-eyed boy to see for him, and the boy has a rosy apple; the crouching mother in the *Mother and Child* (1902) has a baby, and the baby's head is as red as the rose that the same despairing mother carried as she walked by the sea: *Mother and Child at the Seashore* (1902). There is a flush on the feverish face of *The Sick Child* (1903), and the shawl across the boy's shoulders has a rosy cast in *The Tragedy* (1903).

The later barefoot beggar *Boy with Dog* (1905), who is soon recast as a performer, has a mongrel as forlorn as himself, and the dog is like one Picasso once owned— a symbol of fidelity. Just as before, as in a prelude to blue, the little child held a dove:

*Child with Dove* (1901), and the dove was life, while the whole world lay at the child's feet in a ball of many colors. In *The Gourmet* (1901), life is the contents of the pudding bowl the greedy child is devouring.

The Blue Period has another aspect that is poignantly revealed as we view the sad mothers and solemn children born of it. Here, in *La Soupe* (1902), the bowl of soup is carried like a holy object. The *Mother and Child* (1901) praying together inspires awe by its very simplicity. These are religious pictures: the child is always the Child, and the mother is always Mary. Blue is the symbolic color of the Blessed Mother. Her robe, like that little child's, was blue.

Blue is one of Picasso's supreme moments of truth. "Blue so gracious," as he once called it, was the truth as he felt it, at this time; as he lived it, saw it, and transmitted it to us through his art.

*Mother and Child*
*1901    Oil    36×23¾"*
*Mr. and Mrs. William Goetz, Los Angeles*

Mother and Child
1902    Oil    44¼ × 38½"
*Fogg Art Museum, Harvard University*
*Maurice Wertheim Collection*


Left
*Mother and Son at a Fountain*
1901    Oil    16 × 12⅞"
*The Dial Collection*
*on loan at The Worcester Art Museum*


La Soupe
1902    Oil    14⅝ × 17¾"
*Mr. and Mrs. Harold Crang, Toronto*

*Left*
*The Tragedy*
*1903    Oil    42 × 28"*
*National Gallery of Art, Washington, D.C.*
*Chester Dale Collection*

*Mother and Child at the Seashore*
*1902    Oil    32¾ × 23¾"*
*Private Collection, New York*

*Facing page*
*The Sick Child*
*1903    Gouache    18×16"*
*Barcelona, Museum of Modern Art*

*Family Supper*
*1903    Pen, ink, watercolor    12½×17"*
*Albright-Knox Art Gallery, Buffalo*

# 5    *The Circus into Rose*

Once a week the writers and artists had a rendezvous at the Cirque Médrano on the Boulevard de Rochechouart, in Montmartre, where they lived.

They would have gone more often—but once a week was all they could afford. Then the young men and women, artists and models, came out of their tumbledown studios and rooms to enjoy the performing acrobats, tumblers, equestrians, trapeze artists, and clowns. Here in Montmartre the great clowns Grock and Antonet, the American Emmet Kelly, and the Fratellini brothers had become famous. If Grock was performing, Picasso went three times a week.

In those streets, below the Sacré-Cœur, artists and workingmen, milliners and poets, lived side by side. Picasso was passionately in love with the circus: its pageantry and shabby splendor replaced the ritual of the regular Sunday visit to the bullfight in his childhood. He could not get enough of it. When he saw the performance with his friends, he sat spellbound or completely abandoned himself like a child, laughing uproariously. Then he went alone, searching out the performers. He looked for them in the shabby rooms where they lived, in the little restaurants where they ate, in the cafés where they sat between shows, even bringing them home to dinner. Feverishly he painted them.

During his Circus Period, Picasso was more than ever a storyteller. He covers circus life with fidelity: the beginning, the middle, the end. In no other group of paintings does this show more clearly. Here, he becomes the undisputed master of narrative. Life unfolds from birth in the *Harlequin Family* (1905) to *Death of Harlequin* (1905), painted on the reverse of an earlier *Woman Seated in a Garden*. When *Death of*

*Mother and Child*
*1904    Oil    41 × 28½"*
*Private Collection, Paris*

55

*Harlequin* was sold by Somerset Maugham at Sotheby's in 1962, they say a French stockbroker bought the painting and took it to Cannes but rumors persist that it was Picasso himself.

Since it was the drama of life that concerned him, what more dramatic form could it take than the circus with its pretended laughter and real tears beneath its skills—daring and dangerous—dedicated to creating an illusion? The circus was life, and life was the circus.

Fernande Olivier, the red-headed girl who had come into his life, also brought color into Picasso's canvases. He changed his workingman's costume somewhat, though he still wore blue. A white shirt could be seen beneath the open, faded blue jacket and a fringed red-flannel cummerbund topped the blue pants.

For Picasso this was his outer costume, but when he painted Harlequin, he outlined his own features on the white face. He did this many times, through many periods. Later, wherever Harlequin diamonds appeared, there was Picasso himself—they were his private symbols through the Cubist Period. The white face turns up in such strange and different places: as gift to a child still unborn—Paulo, 1921; as image in a mirror in a painting still to be painted—*Las Meninas* (1957). But now he was learning to inhabit Harlequin and to improvise beneath the mask, even as Harlequin must.

Daily life goes on amid the pretended laughter and the tragedy of the performers. Dead-white make-up removed reveals a tender father. Strip the performing child of his droll and colorful costumes, and he has all the characteristics of the impoverished and barefoot ones: he is just a bit more slender, a bit more ethereal, a bit more wistful.

The child that sits besides the old performer in *Acrobat with a Child* (undated) is like a tractable trained dog: both actors are less important than the mysterious box of magic held by the crowned old king of the jesters.

That boy standing with one hand petting his dog while the other holds a half-eaten apple, *Boy with Dog* (1905), later sits stonily beside his mother in the *Artists* (1905). He has lost all taste for food: his face is more mournful here than in *Death of Harlequin*.

56

The Artists, a deep rose picture is back to back with one of a somber crouching figure from the Blue Period, *Girl on the Wall* (1902).

We see these circus people living their pitiful reality while they prepare their various acts, both acts of life and acts of make-believe: holding a baby and putting on make-up; doing the laundry and balancing a ball; fondling a child; waiting for a cue—all studies for the biggest painting Picasso had done so far, the *Saltimbanques* (1905), the only one of three planned large circus compositions that he completed. Picasso had exhausted the theme in his studies.

*Little Girl on Horse*
1905    *Pen drawing*    9⅜ × 12⅛″
*Baltimore Museum of Art*
*Cone Collection*

Saltimbanques
1905    Oil    84×90⅜"
National Gallery of Art, Washington, D.C.
Chester Dale Collection

Upper Right
Boy's Head
1905    Gouache    20×16¼"
Baltimore Museum of Art, Cone Collection

Lower Right
Clown and Boy
1905    Mixed media    23⅝×18½"
Baltimore Museum of Art, Cone Collection

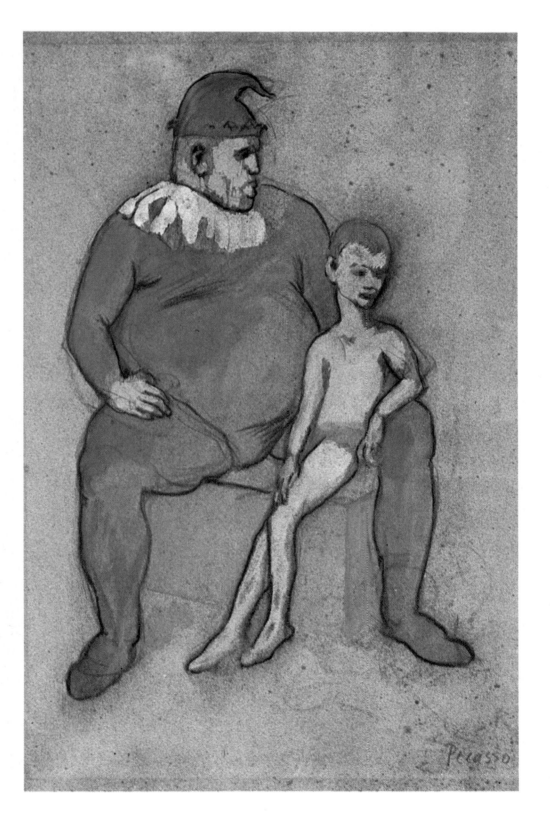

Behind the mask and under the costume, Picasso caught his models about to act, ready to move on—to the next performance, place, time, to the end, each study penetrating one more secret of the story. He identified with their precarious existence; like himself, they, too, lived by skills. They were artists.

The poet Rilke meditated upon the "loveliest Picasso," the *Saltimbanques,* when he lived beside it in Munich, where it once hung. To Rilke, the relationship of these acrobats one to another was symbolic of human relations as a whole. Life was a journey, and the *Saltimbanques* were the travelers.

Rilke saw the tear in the eye of the small boy, sad with "a pain that was still quite small," looking tenderly toward his "seldomly tender mother." Yet, Picasso showed elsewhere, in the two *maternités* of 1904 and 1905 and in the *Acrobat's Family with Ape* (1905), that this same mother could be quite tender. To the boy of the Circus Period the search goes on in the family as the family of wanderers go on forever, searching.

While Picasso himself inhabited the Harlequin's masquerade, the poet Guillaume Apollinaire is often spoken of as the model for the fat clown, the father figure. The Rose Period emerged from the golden aura of Fernande Olivier's hair. The Circus and the Rose Periods overlapped, and introduced a rosier world. Soon the circus was left behind, and the subjects became sturdier, stronger as the color became sunnier.

*Child and Acrobat*
*Undated    Tempera    40×28"*
*Kunsthaus, Zurich*

*Two Acrobats with Dog*
*1905  Gouache  41¼ × 29½″*
*The Hon. and Mrs. William A. Burden,*
*New York*

*Left*
*Little Girl with Dog*
*1905  Gouache  28 × 19¼″*
*Mr. and Mrs. William Goetz, Los Angeles*

*Right*
*Boy with Dog*
*1905  Gouache  22⅜ × 16⅜″*
*Hermitage Museum, Leningrad*

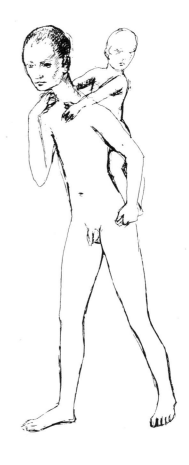

Two Brothers
1905    Ink sketch    12 × 9⅜"
Baltimore Museum of Art
Cone Collection

Left
Two Boys
1905    Watercolor    9⅜ × 7"
Thannhauser Foundation, New York

Right
Two Brothers
1905    Oil    56⅜ × 38⅜"
Kunstmuseum, Basel

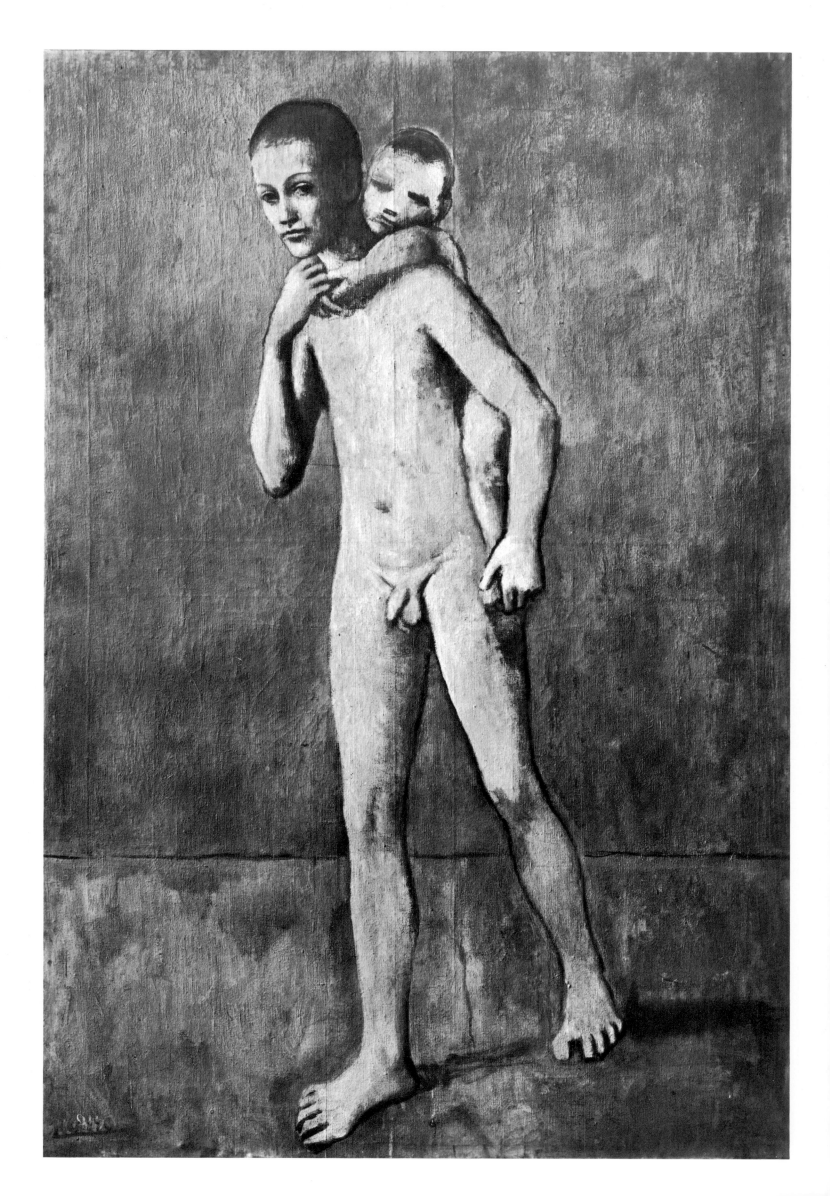

*Facing page*
*Acrobat with a Ball*
*1905    Oil    57⅞ × 37½"*
*Pushkin Museum of*
*Decorative Arts, Moscow*

*Circus Family*
*1905    Pen and watercolor    9½ × 12"*
*Baltimore Museum of Art*
*Cone Collection*

Left
*Harlequin Family*
1905    Ink and gouache    23 × 17¼"
Mr. and Mrs. Julian C. Eisenstein,
Washington, D.C.

*Acrobat's Family with Ape*
1905    Tempera    41 × 29½"
Gothenburg Art Gallery

*Facing page*
*Maternity*
*1905    Gouache    25½ × 19¾"*
*Private Collection, Paris*


*Mother and Child*
*1904    Crayon    13½ × 10½"*
*Fogg Art Museum, Harvard University*
*Meta and Paul J. Sachs Collection*

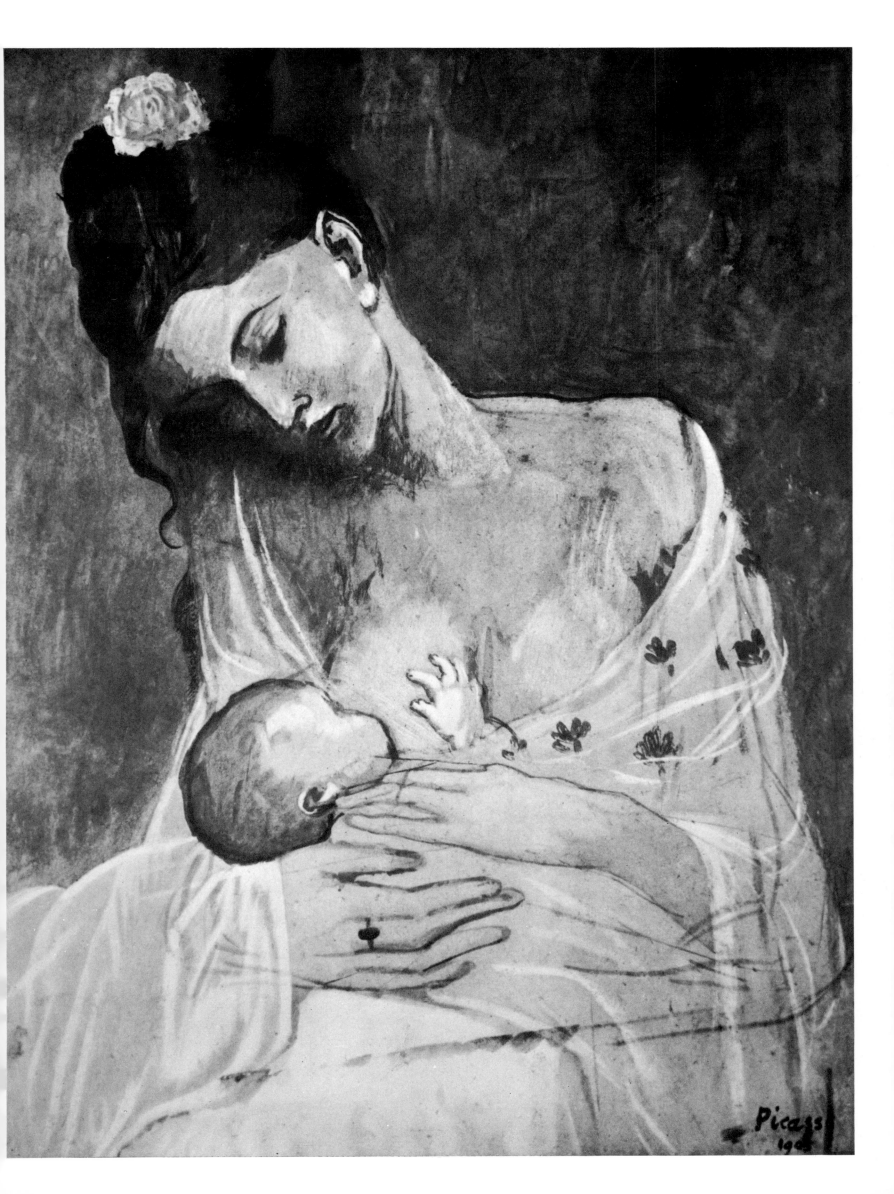

# 6    *"All that was just sentiment"*

The Rose Period began with the promise of success and ended with a "prophecy" of suicide.

An ex-clown, Clovis Sagot, moved into a chemist's shop on the rue Laffitte. Some people have referred to it as an art gallery, but those with longer memories say that it was a glorified junkshop presided over by an "old fox without scruples and without pity." Here Leo Stein found the *Young Girl with a Basket of Flowers* (1905), a blue-and-rose picture of adolescence. His sister Gertrude did not like it at first, but eventually it passed into her collection. They paid 150 francs for it—about thirty dollars at the 1905 rate—and then together visited the young artist in his studio in the Bateau Lavoir, and bought more Picassos for 800 francs.

At this time Picasso met other wealthy Americans, who came to buy pictures, including the sisters Claribel and Etta Cone, the first a medical doctor engaged in research at Johns Hopkins Medical School, the other a collector of textiles. Both were independently wealthy spinsters and were heiresses to a large North Carolina textile fortune. Dr. Claribel, an early suffragette, had gone off to medical school at Harvard with her cousin Gertrude Stein, who later abandoned science for literature, and it was in Gertrude's Paris apartment that Dr. Claribel began her art collection with the purchase of a Matisse. A fine representation of Picasso's early work began with the purchase of a handful of drawings for 100 francs. Such were the modest origins of the great Cone collection, which was added to by the sisters and their bachelor brother Fred.

Picasso was amused to exchange the sisters' gifts of American comics for many

*Death of Harlequin*
*1905    Gouache    26×36⅝"*

73

quick studies that he had intended to throw out. Picasso's clear and curious eye saw the worth in this indigenous form that "The Miss Etta Cones," as he called them, carefully cut out and collected for him. They were reminiscent of the Spanish *aleluyas*, beloved of his childhood, small garish religious prints with the word *aleluya* on them, tossed among the people at Easter Eve. With his facility for using the familiar and the ordinary, refashioning both into art, Picasso considered this a fair exchange.

The Cones mailed to Picasso, or, on yearly visits to Paris, brought him the comic supplements from American Sunday newspapers; these he especially prized because of their strident color and use of frames in rapid sequence. Besides the many pictures they bought, the sisters were allowed to ransack his wastebasket for the throwaways that were later to become priceless. In this way, some of Picasso's most sensitive drawings of children became the property of the Baltimore Museum of Art.

In 1905, many patrons and purchasers haunted Picasso's studio at the Bateau Lavoir. After two exhibitions, Pablo Picasso was known. The poet Guillaume Apollinaire was singing his praises in a review of his work for *La Plume* (May 18, 1905). The wealthy merchant Sergei Shchukine was to buy many Blue Period paintings and carry them back to Moscow in the formative years of his great collection, later nationalized. Picasso had patrons, now, yet as always he painted what he wished. But he also had a commission.

A likeness of the boy Allan Stein (1906), nephew of Gertrude, proved easier to capture than his massive aunt. Picasso asked her to pose for him; she complied— eighty times. He destroyed all the results. His style and Gertrude's face were at war. Picasso was caught up in the tentative activities of a great transition.

Fortunately, Ambroise Vollard offered to represent him and gave him 2000 francs as an advance on a large group of pictures. Picasso went off to Gosol, in the Pyrenees. Here, as he vacationed in the wild Andorra valley, he meditated on the new direction that his art was taking. He was inspired by the ancient Iberian bronzes he found in Spain as well as by the African masks he had recently been introduced to in Paris. Through them he came to his new vision. One immediate result was that on his return,

Picasso knew how to solve the problem of Gertrude Stein's portrait. He worked without the model, from memory, and gave the painting to her (1906).

The more important missing ingredient that solved Picasso's technical dilemma was African art, the essentials of which he used for his own ends. The bold distortion of Negro art, with its sense of the tragic and the mysterious, together with its often naive and childlike humor, appealed to him.

Picasso's masklike portrait of Gertrude Stein has also become her public image. "For me, it is I," she said, "and it is the only reproduction of me which is always I for me."

Of Picasso's work itself, she said: "After that, little by little his drawing hardened, his line became firmer, his color more vigorous, naturally, he was no longer a boy, he was a man."

*Les Demoiselles d'Avignon* (1907), the young ladies of the Carrer d'Avinyó in Barcelona, a pivotal work that was to lead him into new fields, completely absorbed him now. Aiming to eliminate mood from his paintings, he was led gradually into Cubism. *Les Demoiselles d'Avignon* is one of the few paintings in which the canvas itself is the battleground of the past and the future. The three figures to the left belong to Picasso's past: they are of the Rose Period (even though they may seem to be parodies of it); those on the right tell of his obsession with the problem of how to construct the human form. The right side is Cubism itself.

Here was a new way of seeing, through shape and geometric pattern. It was shocking—a bold turning off into new paths. The actual confrontation of tradition and invention within the confines of a single canvas added to the shocking aspects of *Les Demoiselles*. The painting puzzled and mystified Picasso's friends, among them his most daring colleagues, not excluding Braque, who later disciplined Cubism like an inspired schoolmaster.

Those who visited Picasso's studio to see the painting, considered it a fiasco. Leo Stein called it monstrous. Others laughed behind his back; his dealers warned him that the new style would not sell, and departed. But Picasso had to find his own way.

In this trying time, Picasso acquired a new dealer, the youthful Daniel-Henry Kahnweiler, who left the financial world into which he had been born, to become the representative of the revolutionary young artists.

"I did not know anyone. I was twenty-two years old, and I arrived from London to sell paintings." This was in 1907. He had visited the Salon d'Automne and had gone to the front doors of several galleries "of which I did not dare to cross the threshold."

But he did dare to back Pablo Picasso, who was but four years older than he. He was convinced of the value of Picasso's new experiments, even in the face of hearing the painter André Derain predict that some day Picasso would hang himself behind his great canvas.

Shocked by his friends' reactions, Picasso left the work unfinished. The painting was not shown, except to those who visited his studio. For years, the canvas lay rolled up and was eventually (after 1920) bought sight unseen. It did not appear in print until 1925, when the Cubist experiments had run their course; it was then reproduced in a new review, *La Révolution Surréaliste,* though Picasso was never a true surrealist. In 1937, during the Paris International Exposition, it was shown publicly for the first time at the Petit Palais. The Museum of Modern Art of New York bought it in 1939 and exhibited it later that year.

Speaking of his pre-revolutionary paintings, Picasso once said, "All that was just sentiment"—an innovator's disclaimer.

Apollinaire, recognizing the magic for what it was, described it precisely, in *Les Lettres Modernes* (1905). "Everything enchants him, and his undeniable talent seems to me to serve an imagination in which the delightful and the horrible, the low and the delicate, are proportionately mingled."

As the master painter of Cubism, the central problem of which is structure, Picasso had little time for children in the long years from 1907 to 1921. Only after his marriage of 1918 did he once again take a brief side glance at the charms of other people's children.

76

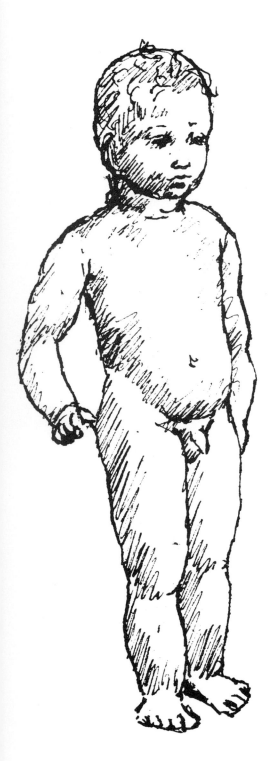

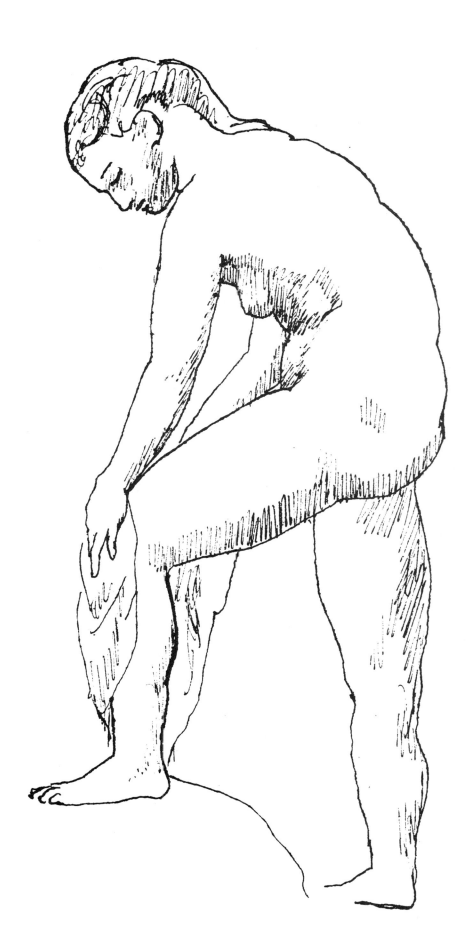

*Mother and Son*
*1906   Ink sketch    11 ½ × 19 ½"*
*Galerie Louise Leiris, Paris*

Picasso painted and sketched the wife and family of the art dealer Paul Rosenberg in Paris and also at Biarritz in 1918, where the two friends lived side by side and vacationed together; but these were done in his nonrevolutionary style. He also gave them a pencil drawing of the small Rosenberg child in a nurse's uniform, as a pretended *Infirmière* (1919), along with a sketch of the little girl struggling with an enormous rabbit, hugged tightly; both child and rabbit are quite determined. There are others of the Rosenberg children, all cherished family souvenirs.

These pictures of children were made when Picasso was again using a classic style for figures. Yet he did paint a few cubist children. In 1919, a little girl and her hoop fascinated him, and versions of this remain among his rare ventures into the realm of childhood during the Cubist Period. There are two such canvases: one is small, with the hoop centered; the other is larger, with the hoop at the lower left. Flat as playing cards and strongly colored, here the child is seen in relation to familiar symbols of childhood. But for these, the child during Cubism was all but forgotten.

Picasso was to speak of childhood in a firmer voice, passionately and unabashedly tender, and in all styles and media, in the deeply personal days to come.

*Boy Leading a Horse*
*1905    Oil    86½ × 51¼"*
*Mr. and Mrs. William S. Paley, New York*

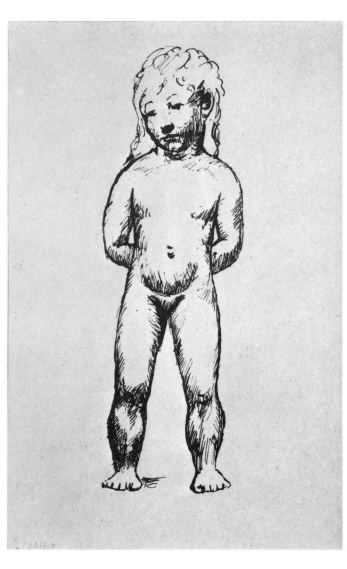

*Little Girl*
*1906    Pen    15 × 10½"*
*Baltimore Museum of Art*
*Cone Collection*

*Right*
*Child Playing*
*1906    Drawing    11⅜ × 7½"*
*Baltimore Museum of Art*
*Cone Collection*

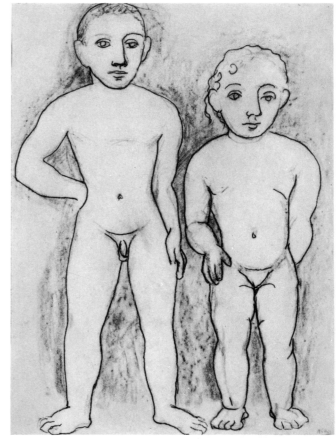

*Two Nude Children*
*1906    Crayon and pastel    24¾ × 19"*

*Left*
*Mother and Daughter*
*1904    Crayon    11 × 14"*
*Fogg Art Museum, Harvard University*
*Maurice Wertheim Collection*

*Left*
*Head of a Boy*
*1906    Oil    14×9″*
*Mme Helena Rubinstein, New York*

*Portrait of Allan Stein*
*1906    Gouache    29⅛×23½″*
*Baltimore Museum of Art*
*Cone Collection*

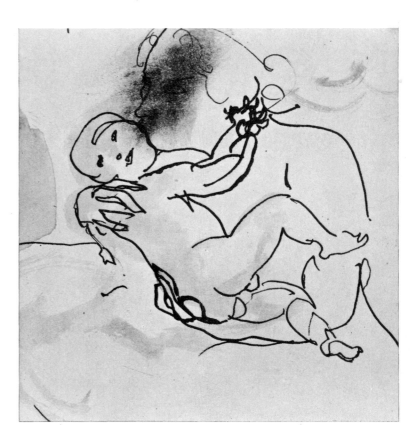

# 7 *The Mammoth Mothers*

How does the child see his mother? Is she not a Giantess to her child?

The mammoth mother was the child of the Neoclassic Period, inspired by ancient Greece, by ancient Rome, and by romance—and by the elegant line of a dancer's body.

After 1916 Picasso had begun to use Cubism for still lifes; the classic style he reserved for his figures. In 1917, Jean Cocteau invited Picasso to design sets for the Russian ballet, then in Rome. There the environment replenished his new trend: both the classic setting and the traditional art form of the dance. Picasso fell in love with Olga Koklova, a member of the *corps de ballet,* and married her the following year.

Begun in elegance, the Neoclassic Period burst into life, was climaxed by the mammoth mothers, and receded to the normal condition of the elegant line. Picasso thus followed the cycle of pregnancy itself. All fluid form and line, the dancer's body, an instrument of art, had been distorted by the maturing fetus, an instrument of life.

On February 4, 1921, Olga gave birth to a boy, and once again Picasso was inspired to sing in praise of motherhood. The following summer, after his son's birth, Picasso painted many giant earth symbols. The women were ponderous, more fleshy, a muchness of woman, bloated with life, like antique statues suddenly given life. They were, like all Great Mothers, grounded to the earth, enormous.

At least a dozen of these mammoth mothers exist. Though some of the canvases are not large in themselves, the effect of any one of them is of something so much larger than life as to seem gigantic. The biggest of them all, *Woman and Child* (1921), is at the Chicago Institute of Art. It was originally called *Maternité au bord de la mer,* since the mother sits by the sea like the Blue Period *Mother and Child at the Seashore*

*Little Girl with a Hoop*
*1919    Oil    56×31"*
*Eva Gebhard Foundation, New York and*
*The Baroness Gourgaud, Paris*

(1902) walked by the shore. Life continued to ebb and flow with the tide, though Picasso's figures were no longer victims, but powerful and flowing models, like ancient goddesses that no tide could touch. They were nourishing mothers, ugly and beautiful. Sometimes the distortions narrowly bordered on the monstrous. Absorbed with this delicate balance between the ugly and beautiful, he magically made both into art.

The swollen and the oversized had often fascinated Picasso. At one time he worked on a series of mammoth sculptures, hoping to have them permanently placed on the Croisette in Cannes along with the giant African palms—but no one ever offered him the boulevard.

In the mammoth mothers, Picasso sees as the child sees: the world is the mother, and the mother is the world. In the beginning the boundaries are the mother's arms. They make a unity, an island. The mammoth mother herself is female cousin to those male island guardians, the solemn giant grotesques of Easter Island.

As with infants, so, too, with infant societies. Among all early cultures, the female goddess dominated. The mother image, then, must be of mammoth size.

As Picasso displays them, in quiet tones of gray and rose, the mammoth mothers give comfort. The naked, lusty baby in the arms of a strong mother—for the baby also is a giant (there is a canvas of the oversized infant alone with the mother's lap as background)—affords reason enough for the serenity of form and face of a modern-day fertility symbol.

*Maternity*
*1921   Oil   60⅔ × 41"*

88

*Maternity*
*1921   Oil   60⅔ × 41″*

*The Family*
*1923   Sanguine and oil   27¾ × 41¾″*
*Thannhauser Foundation, New York*

Mother and Child
1921    Pencil    9¾ × 12¼"
Cleveland Museum of Art
Mr. and Mrs. Lewis B. Williams Collection

Left
Maternity
1921    Oil    25¾ × 18¼"
The Abrams Family Collection, New York

Right
Woman and Child
1921    Oil    56½ × 64"
Art Institute of Chicago

*Mother and Child*
*1924    Aquatint    22½ × 30"*
*Galerie Louise Leiris, Paris*

*Left*
*Mother and Child*
*1922    Oil    39½ × 31½"*
*The Hon. and Mrs. W. Averell Harriman,*
*New York*

# 8   *The Family Gallery*

*Avers: ni signature*
*ni date*
*Revers: date 1-14-23*

When a picture appears in a gallery catalogue with such comments as the above, it is a reminder that the picture is Picasso's very own. It is not for sale: it is exhibited only to allow a quick look into the artist's heart. These are pictures from Picasso's family album. They include his children: Paulo, born in 1921, Maya in 1935, Claude in 1947, and Paloma in 1949. Most of these paintings are unsigned. A date is written on the back for family identification, but not always.

Picasso calls these representations of his own flesh and blood the "Family Gallery." They are a father's souvenirs of his children as they were yesterday, not today.

The Family Gallery hangs here and there in the various houses Picasso has lived in over the years. Mostly the pictures are stored in the attics and studios that he filled with his work before moving on: at the rue des Grands-Augustins, at Vallauris, and at Cannes, and at other houses he has lived in and left behind. These places are closed, yet cleaned and tended; even though they are used as warehouses, they remain as he left them, because he just might be back sometime to finish what he had begun there. And they may become museums.

Many pictures from the Family Gallery were shown for the first time at the Salon d'Automne in 1944 after the liberation of Paris, when Picasso exhibited eighty works in a gallery set apart for him alone. In 1949, pictures of his new family were shown at the Maison de la Pensée Française in Paris; the subjects were Claude Gilot Picasso and his mother, Françoise Gilot. More of the Family Gallery went on view in Rome and Milan in 1953; a few pictures appeared at the Musée des Arts Décoratifs in Paris in 1955 (where two-year-old Paulo Picasso's face was the poster on the door-and-lamp-post advertising of that exhibition); additional ones were in the New York Museum of Modern Art show in 1957; the greatest number were assembled at the Tate Gallery, London in 1960; a group went to Poland in 1962. But the Family Gallery has never been seen anywhere as a whole.

Paulo Picasso owns one picture from the Family Gallery: his portrait at the age of two, *The Artist's Son* (1923). Claude Gilot Picasso received a picture from his father as a gift—the first for his own collection. The dog Jan is included in the family portrait of *Claude and Paloma with their Mother* (1951).

Pictures of the Picasso children are not for sale—yet, there are exceptions to this rule. Behind the family paintings in other collections there is always a special story.

Two paintings, nearly alike, of Paulo and his mother, *Mother and Child* (1922), were sold when Picasso's marriage to Olga was breaking up. In fact, at that time Picasso stopped painting altogether for a full year.

Three others that have left home, *Paloma Asleep* (1952), *Figures in a Garden from a Window* (1953-54), and *Two Children* (1956) throw some light on what keeps a picture exclusively in the Family Gallery.

*Paloma Asleep* (1952) has a sculptural quality and is painted in tones of steel. It could be that of any child asleep and it cuts knife-sharp into the heart. It could leave the Family Gallery, because Paloma inspired the painting, but it was not a portrait.

In *Two Children* (1956) the children are playing in the garden, but their faces are merely circled, suggested, as in *Figures in a Garden from a Window* (1953-54), and neither are portraits. The figure of the artist in the gloom of the studio with the children in the light of the garden during that sad holiday season was painted at the close of one year and the beginning of the new, a time when the hurt of Françoise Gilot's decision to leave was too sharp to bear, and the painting was too painful a reminder to keep.

The tangled story of Paulo's portraits as Harlequin or Pierrot discloses most about Picasso's attitude toward the paintings of his children. It unravels slowly and reveals Picasso's pain at parting with the pictures of his children.

*Paulo as Pierrot with Flowers* (1929) was said to be no longer in Picasso's possession. The story was told that it had been given to a doctor who took care of Paulo as a child, because the doctor had asked for it, and that it ultimately had become the property of Mr. and Mrs. William Goetz of California. However, when the present owners granted permission to reproduce what was now their painting of the costumed Paulo, they called their picture by a different name, and dated it differently: *Paulo as Harlequin with Flowers* (1923). Were there then two similar paintings, painted at different times?

There were two: one had left the Family Gallery—the other was still Picasso's.

The provenance of the Harlequin painting verified four owners: Picasso who had painted it, Dr. A. Gosset of Paris, then his widow, and now Mr. and Mrs. William Goetz. Picasso still owned the Pierrot.

Here was a confusion and a mystery. Who was Dr. Gosset? Was this a gift for routine pediatric care? Why did those who should know think that Dr. Gosset owned a picture which had really remained in Picasso's possession all these years?

Both pictures were indeed similar: the same stance, the same flower in the hat and on the cane, and the same big bouquet in the chubby hand. The costumes, though, were different: one was clearly a Harlequin with red and blue colors boldly streaking the masquerade, while the 1929 painting was dead-white and very like the *Paulo as Pierrot with Mask* (1925). There were differences in the color background; one was pale green, the other a sunnier yellow. Further, there was something amorphous, suggestive, about the earlier Harlequin painting which seemed to indicate a freer hand, while the later one was more studied—in keeping with the others in the Harlequin-Pierrot series, painted on birthdays, as souvenirs of celebrations.

Other discrepancies related to life itself immediately became visible. Though six years separated them—a long time in a child's life—Picasso had not registered the signs of maturing, signs to which he was most sensitive. The Pierrot was supposed to have been painted on July 12, 1929, when Paulo was eight-and-a-half years old, yet the boy did not look like an eight-year-old. The Harlequin, on the other hand, was said to have been painted on a second birthday in February, 1923, and Paulo had lost all the round youngness shown in pictures belonging to that same period. One had to be a copy of the other. Which was the earlier?

Of course, Picasso frequently made many studies with only slight variations; one may have been a sketch, another an aquatint, a pastel, an ink drawing, an oil painting, a lithograph. He did many versions of the same essential subject from different points of view, using different angles of observation. These facts did not seem to solve the puzzle of the Harlequin-Pierrot. Why were there two—and so nearly alike? Why were they painted over such a long span of time?

It is common knowledge that there were occasions when an individual asked Picasso for a certain picture—to exhibit, sell or publish—and Picasso, in his disordered order, could not or would not take the time to find it. Instead, he quickly made another, which was a solution for both the asker and the giver. In a way, that is what happened with the two masquerade pictures: the Pierrot and the Harlequin.

In July, 1929, when Paulo was eight-and-a-half years old he caught his hand in a slammed door, and Dr. Antoine Gosset came to sew up his finger. When asked his fee, the attending surgeon requested Paulo's picture, which hung in the nursery. Reluctantly Picasso parted with the picture, dating it from memory —1923— as it left the studio. Annoyed at having to give up a picture from the Family Gallery, Picasso immediately painted another to keep among his souvenirs. At the time, he dated the completed work of *Paulo as Pierrot with Flowers* (1929), but it was as he remembered Paulo at the age of four. When it appeared in the 1953 Italian show, Picasso called it: *Paulo, Son of the Artist, at the Age of Four with a Bouquet of Flowers* (1929). Both pictures were of Paulo at four: one a payment for medical service, the other a replacement for the Family Gallery. Otherwise the Family Gallery remains at home.

*Paulo*  The portraits Picasso devoted to his first-born son Paulo are among the tenderest ever painted of a child. His visual record of Paulo's childhood has certain characteristics all its own. Full of playfulness and fantasy and make-believe, it shows the child as plaything, playmate, and toy, the infant of the storybook. He interprets his small subject in the classic tradition, with the boy as little shepherd, as Harlequin, as Pierrot. Paulo's portraits radiate pure wonderment and joy.

Pablo Picasso gave his son a name from his own long necklace of names. After all, Pablo is the Spanish for Paul.

He painted his son realistically, yet with sentiment and adoration; on the day he was born, at two weeks, at one month, on birthdays and in between. He sketched him lying on a pillow, drinking from a bottle, and in his mother's arms. He painted Paulo toddling with a plush toy horse in his hands at twenty months, and then metamorphosed him into a small shepherd with a lamb (1923). From a photograph of Paulo on a burro, the kind every photographer made for every parent as a keepsake, he painted a realistic picture. Then he enlarged the head into a touching portrait of a two-year-old, later used as a poster for Picasso's 1955 show at the Musée des Arts Décoratifs. He painted Paulo as Pierrot in the same sort of Pierrot costume that Renoir had used in painting his son Jean. He painted Paulo as *torero* and, of course, as Harlequin, sharing his private masquerade with his son. He liked Paulo as Harlequin so much that he painted that head separately, too, in a tender close-up. Then he made another, less personal picture, *Harlequin as a Child* (1927), the line and mask covering the child's face.

Except for the burro, all of Paulo's animals are toys. In later years Picasso again began to use the dog as a protective symbol, a companion for his young children, just as in his early pictures of the poor and the circus children the animal had symbolized fidelity. Somehow he missed putting Bob, the big St. Bernard, friend of the 1920's into a picture. Sketches of Elft, a favorite of 1936, must be filed somewhere. Later dogs fared better: Kazbek, an Afghan hound, often with Maya; Jan, a boxer, nursemaid of Paloma and Claude; Lump, a dachshund, a gift from David Duncan, immortalized in *Las Meninas* (1957). Perro, just "dog" in Spanish, a Dalmatian, appears in more recent pictures; here the name also sounds like Pierrot, and the puppy was a clown. Picasso is an incorrigible punster. Then there was Kaboul, still another Afghan hound.

There were always animals around, in addition to the ever-present pigeons: a pet owl, *Hibou Perché* (1947), with eyes as wide and wise as Picasso's own, and *Grand Hibou* (1948); and a goat called She, though a male, sculptured into a statue (1950), to whose sturdy tail the live goat was frequently tied. They say it slept outside Picasso's door at Vallauris.

When Paulo was a boy, the house was too formal for all that. Olga Koklova, his mother, ran it on solid bourgeois lines. She was the daughter of a White Russian general and she kept the nursery far from the studio. Yet Picasso painted Paulo's furniture and even fashioned his toys. Then he borrowed them for his paintings. He decorated the nursery furniture with simple patterns and scrolls. We can see the toy theater he made for Paulo in *The Studio* (1925), an oil painted at Juan-les-Pins. But the day he contrived a surprise for Paulo by designing Harlequin cushions for his new toy car was a sad one. Paulo wept; he wanted the car as it had been.

This fascination with cars as they had been continued into Paulo Picasso's adult life. He became a collector of old cars. Among others he owned a Voisin, 1920. When he was very young he liked motorcycles and later racing cars. At one time he acted as chauffeur for his father in the old Hispano-Suiza, also of the twenties, which had "many comforts" and was souped-up so that he could drive his father from Paris to

*Paulo as Pierrot with Flowers*
*1929    Oil    51×38"*

Cannes at 140 kilometers an hour "without even trying," they say. The old car had been with them for so long that it was treated lovingly—like a member of the family. Parting with it was difficult, but when driving it became a daily risk, it was retired like an old pensioner, and a Hotchkiss replaced it for workaday chores.

Later, Picasso was given a white Oldsmobile convertible by an American art dealer, and Paulo arrived at Vallauris for his father's eightieth birthday celebration in the old Hispano-Suiza, brought out to share in the festivities. Mostly Paulo drove a fast convertible, looking like a professional racer, his cigarette held in a vertical position.

The companionship of the father and his first-born continued through years that were often difficult. Even when Paulo was only two, Picasso carried him proudly to watch rehearsals of the ballet *The Blue Train*. Later, he would borrow him from the English governess and take him to the bullfights, just as his own father Don José had carried away his own small son long years ago. Even now Paulo rushes down from Paris to enjoy the bullfights with "le père" at Arles, since Picasso does not go to Spain. Paulo is also an *aficionado* of the arena.

During the time Picasso needed solitude and all his energies to grapple with the details of his mural *War and Peace* (1952), only Paulo was allowed to watch the work in progress, when he brought him to work at the abandoned perfume factory that was the studio in Vallauris, and called for him late at night. Picasso needed the companionship of his son during the long and late hours he worked; it was a time of closeness for both.

Before either Paulo or Maya were married and they were with their father, it was they who would pick up the check or pay the bill when they were together in public places, since Picasso never carried cash.

Paulo was the best man at his father's marriage to Jacqueline Roque at the Vallauris *mairie* in the spring of 1961. He also represents his father on such sad occasions as the funeral of Jean Cocteau, in October, 1963.

Paulo gave Picasso his first grandchildren when the son married the daughter of a garage owner from Golfe Juan, the twin seaside town of the hilltop village of

*Paulo as Harlequin with Flowers*
*1923    Oil    36½ × 28½″*
*Mr. and Mrs. William Goetz, Los Angeles*
*Reproduced courtesy of "Art News"*

Vallauris. A boy and a girl were born of this marriage: Pablo Picasso II and Marina. They are but a few years younger than Claude and Paloma, their own aunt and uncle. They live with their mother, while Paulo now lives with his second wife, Christine of the brilliant black eyes, on the street of the old dovecot, the rue du Vieux-Colombier in Paris. They have a small boy, Bernard, born in 1959, and a friendly dog with a Hebrew name, Yona. "It means pigeon, too," Christine explained.

To this day, next to Paulo's bed stands the greenish chest with scrolls and decorations that his father made for him as a child. The portrait of Paulo hangs in his living room, along with many penciled sketches of his mother Olga, who died in Cannes in 1955. He looks very much like her, as does his son Bernard, and yet there is something of his paternal grandfather, Don José Ruiz, too—reddish hair and brownish-red eyes.

"Paulo is a sweet boy... a sweet boy," people say of him. He is sensitive, handsome, alert and tender. He and Christine and their little boy exude affection and warmth and youthful yearning.

*Paulo with a Lamb*
*1923    Oil    51 × 38″*

*Left*
*The Artist's Son*
*1923   Oil   10¾ × 8¾″*
*Collection of Paul Picasso*

*Paulo on a Donkey*
*1923   Oil   40 × 32⅜″*

Head of Harlequin
1924    Oil    13½ × 10½"

Left
Paulo as Harlequin
1924    Oil    51 × 38"

Right
Paulo, Aged Two
1923    Oil    52 × 38¾"

Left
*Story Time*
*1926    Lithograph    13 × 9⅞″*
*The Museum of Modern Art, New York*
*Gift of Mrs. John D. Rockefeller*


Right
*Paulo as Pierrot with Mask*
*1925    Oil    51 × 38″*


*The Wooden Horse*
*1926    Pen    16¼ × 19½″*

*Maya* Maya's mother, Marie-Thérèse Walter, had such soft blonde beauty and an air of such detachment that Picasso often painted her as a moonface.

In 1935, a golden-haired baby girl was born. Picasso sketched her dancing, sleeping, clowning. He painted her with a sailor doll, wearing a sailor hat, holding a sailboat, somehow forecasting her future. He sketched her with a rag doll in her hair instead of a ribbon and with her golden braids pinned high. He painted her in the arms of her mother, both realistically and distortedly, as she saw the child up close and as he saw them together, giving both angles of vision, his and hers, simultaneously. Mother and daughter are looking at each other almost as in the game of owl that young children play:

> *Heads together, up so close,*
> *Close your eyes, nose to nose,*
> *Say "owl." Now open. What do you see?*

In the game, the eyes merge into one Cyclopean orb in the middle of the forehead. Then the wide-open eyes move across each other and into the cheeks, one up and one down.

Even Maya's toys were her father's concern. He made her dolls of everything: wood, clay, wire—and surprises. He could contrive all sorts of magic out of paper—dresses, masks, books—just for her. Drawings, of course, and jokes, and things made with chickpeas. He had to improvise desperately, since Maya was a child of the war years.

*Paulo as Torero*
*1925    Oil    63¾ × 38"*

The war began early for Picasso—in Spain. He loved his country passionately. He would not sacrifice his Spanish citizenship; though he had lived permanently in France since his twenties, he chose to remain Spanish always. Torn apart by Civil War, Spain became a testing ground. Picasso used his total resources—words, money, the power of his brush—to defend his motherland.

His old mother, still alive in Barcelona, wrote him of the screams she heard. His passion found formal expression in the great *Guernica* mural (1937), a scream on canvas. He painted a dead child in the arms of a tormented mother, yet he painted Maya as a wiggly little girl, as his delight, reassured that she was still there: "See, I am not only occupied with gloom," he said.

When the rehearsal that was Spain was over and the real war began, Picasso was penned in at No. 7, rue des Grands-Augustins. There was no heat; the studio was freezing; yet he had to paint. His hands stiffened and he could barely move his brush. When the sounds of battles seemed close by, he was busy painting realistic portraits of his daughter, tenderly, to relieve the tension. Maya was life.

Maia, Maja, or Maya, was variously spelled. How did she herself spell it? Now Madame Pierre Widmaier, the wife of a sailor, living in Marseilles with her small son Olivier and her new baby (1964), Maya was her own invention, the name she had given herself as a child. "For who at three can say María?" she asked. Then rhapsodizing on the multiple meanings: "The Mayas of America, Maya meaning water in Arabian and also woman, and meaning "mine" in Russian. I think for a woman it is a very nice name. They called me María de la Concepción because my father had a young sister by this name and because she died at seven.

"The nicest thing about being with my father? We have so much, both, that it is impossible to find one nicer than another. My childhood was during the war and my father would every day find jokes for the little girl I was. Making me drawings, books by himself, funny dresses, etc., dolls—and as you can imagine, he made them with everything. The funniest were of chickpeas. Now I make some for Olivier."

*Maya*
*1938    Aquatint    28½ × 21½"*
*Mr. and Mrs. Aaron Ginsburg, N.Y.*

*Maya*
*1938    Pencil    10¼ × 6¾"*

*Left*
*Maya with Sailboat*
*1938    Oil    28½ × 21"*

*Right*
*Maya and Sailor Doll*
*1938    Oil    29¼ × 24"*

*Maya Dancing*
1942    *Lead drawing*    14 × 8¼"
*Pages from a notebook*

*Right*
*Maya Clowning*
*1942   Lead drawing   13½ × 8″*
*Page from a notebook*

17 juin 43

Maya Sleeping
1938    Pencil    9⅓ × 5½″

Left
Maya with a Rag Doll in Her Hair
1943    Lead drawing    14¼ × 12″

Right
Maya
1943    Charcoal    14¼ × 12″

*Claude* All over the walls of the Grimaldi Museum at Antibes, Picasso drew what he called his *joie de vivre.* Here he develops a new mythology to sing his song to the young, beautiful, and gifted Françoise Gilot and the boy child that was to be born to them. Claude Gilot Picasso was born in 1947, and Picasso, meditating on the poetic theme, made a series of pictorial comments on a frolicking centaur family. The *Birth of the Last Centaur,* an etching, is a more solemn representation.

Claude looks most like his father. He has the same burning eyes, the same hanging forelock. He was born when his father was already sixty-five years old. The Picassos made their home, now, in a square house on top of a hill overlooking Vallauris, a pottery center since Roman days. Claude is the name of the patron saint of Vallauris. Though Picasso's Claude Gilot is named for Watteau's art teacher, a Claude Gillot.

They say Picasso walked up from the seashore one day to ask Georges Ramié and his wife, the potters, if he might work with them. Then he stayed for ten years, transforming the utilitarian village into a bustling art and curio center. In Vallauris, scents had been pressed from the flowers of the hillside almost as long as clay objects had been shaped from the soil. An abandoned perfume factory became his studio. He left his stamp permanently in the deconsecrated twelfth-century chapel with the large mural *War and Peace* (1952); and in the central square, among widespread sycamores stands his statue, *The Man with the Sheep* (1943). On market days, the children play their games around its base—*la ronde des enfants.*

Picasso took up his stylus and scratched directly onto a lithographic stone a poem and a picture of his second son, the "Child of I and the other." Writing with almost

*Maya*
*1943    Lead drawing    14¼ × 12"*
*Page from a notebook*

123

no punctuation, almost without paragraphing, as in old manuscripts, he decorated his block print with erasures and drawings—and rhapsodized. To him a poem and a painting were the same: "You can write a picture in words just as you can paint sensations in a poem," he said.

> *At a quarter to four exactly in full sunshine the Child of I and the other placed on the edge of the window playing with his fingernails and his spots of shadow and light.... The mother a meter 70 centimeters two arms two legs two hands two feet one head two eyes two ears one nose one mouth one stomach hair guts two breasts a navel a bottom a con twenty fingers hairs on the legs on the arms on the bottom on the con veins blood farts urine flesh fat tendons and the belly full of bones. His mother his mama was looking at the child of the I and the other she loved him she gave him the soup of her breast washed him morning and night combed him and sewed his dresses went with him to the movies to the theater to the sea and slapped him Mama Mama I have finished Mama give me a drink Mama I am thirsty Mama I am hungry Mama I am sleepy Do you want me to blow your nose Are you hot are you cold nighty night pipi caca Ah how heavy to carry are the wings of the horse said the I putting down the package on the sink. Neither rain nor shine nor snow and even less the vines in autumn.*

He had painted his picture in words.

Picasso painted Claude as he saw him in a cradle, or in a carriage with his hobby-horse or in his mother's arms. The infant was dressed up in his Polish swaddling clothes just after Picasso attended a peace conference there. In all these pictures the child is as decorative as an old Spanish tile.

Then, just as he had taken Paulo to the bullfights, so he initiated Claude into the life of the arena. The ceramic tile of Claude as *torero* celebrated the annual happy festivities in Vallauris, where the bull is never killed. On the back Picasso wrote "tu," for Claude. Claude also made a special picture for him: *La corrida,* which hung at La Californie: "pour mon papa chéri, Claude."

*Claude in His Bed*
*1948   Oil   51×38"*

AUX TROMPETTES DES SONNERIES
QUI SE COLLAIENT A SES JOUES MORDOREES
DANS LA GLUE DE PATTES DE MOUCHES
DES BULLES DE SAVON DE SES CRIS FON-
DANT LA ROBE ROSE A POIS ROUGES AU
BLANC ARDENT DES PASTILLES ODO-
RANTES DE SES CHEVEUX LE SUCRE
FONDU AU FOND DE LA TASSE ET
TOUT LE PAYSAGE INCLUS A L'
INTERIEUR DES POINGS FERMES
DU SOLEIL - LES FRANGES DU
RIDEAU COUVERT DE PUNAISES
LE DECORANT DECORATIVEMENT
DE BLEU ET DE VERT VERONESE
21

SUINTANT METHODIQUEMENT CACHES ET PRUDEMMENT
MIS SOUS CLOCHE LES MUSIQUES LES FEUX DE
BENGALE ET LES PARFUMS DES MAINS VOL
ANTES DES QUELQUES FLEURS MISES DEBOUT
LEURS PIQUES PIQUEES SUR LA PEAU DU PAIN
RECOUVERT D'ENCRE S'AGITANT FOLLEMENT
DANS LES REGLES DU JEU ET LES CEREMONIES
LES CARESSES LES MENACES LES COUPS
TOUTES LEURS GRIFFES DEHORS IMITANT
TIMIDEMENT L'ORCHESTRE DES DESIRS
ET L'ORPHEON DE DEGOUTS AGITANT DANS
LA SOUPE LEURS LINGES DECHIRES.
LA MERE UN METRE SOIXANTE-DIX DEUX
BRAS DEUX JAMBES DEUX MAINS DEUX PIEDS
UNE TETE DEUX YEUX DEUX OREILLES UN
NEZ UNE BOUCHE UN ESTOMAC DES
CHEVEUX DES TRIPES DEUX MAMELLES
UN NOMBRIL UN CUL UN CON VINGT DOIGTS
22

DES POILS ~~SUR~~ SUR LES JAMBES SUR
LES BRAS SUR LE CUL ET LE CON
DES VEINES DU SANG DES PETS
DE L'URINE DE LA VIANDE DE LA
GRAISSE DES TENDONS ET LE
VENTRE PLEIN D'OS - SA MERE
SA MAMAN ELLE REGARDAIT
L'ENFANT DE L'I ET L'AUTRE
ELLE L'AIMAIT LUI DONNAIT LA
SOUPE DE SE SEINS LE LAVAIT LE
MATIN ET LE SOIR LE PEIGNAIT
ET LUI COUSAIT SES ROBES
ALLAIT AVEC LUI AU CINEMA
AU THEATRE A LA MER

23

ET LUI DONNAIT DES GIFLES
MAMAN MAMAN J'AI FINI
MAMAN DONNE-MOI A BOIRE
MAMAN J'AI SOIF MAMAN J'AI
FAIN MAMAN J'AI SOMMEIL VEUX
-TU QUE JE TE MOUCHE AS-TU
CHAUD AS-TU FROID DODO PIPI
CACA - AH QUE LES AILES DU CHE-
VAL SONT LOURDES A PORTER
DIT L'I DEPOSANT LE PAQUET
SUR L'EVIER - NI LA PLUIE
NI LE BEAU TEMPS NI LA
NEIGE ET ENCORE MOINS
LES VIGNES A L'AUTOMNE

24

*Claude and His Hobbyhorse*
1949   Oil   51×38″

*Satyr, Faun and Centaur*
1946
*Picasso Museum, Antibes*

*Birth of the Last Centaur*
1947   Etching   13½ × 10¼"

*Claude in Blue*
1951    Oil    18 × 14¾″

*Paloma* *Et le ventre plein d'os*—"the belly full of bones"—turned into a baby girl, born in the spring of 1949 at the moment of an international peace meeting in Paris. To the April gathering Picasso announced he would give his new child a romantic Spanish name—Paloma, the dove. Like Claude, she had the dark Picasso eyes.

He did not measure Paloma in exact centimeters as he had her mother Françoise; rather he measured her mercurial spirit, catching it in every motion, gesture, mood, in every flexed muscle, every relaxed and taut limb.

Paloma's babyhood was searched and scanned and transformed into art, much as a scientist might study an amoeba under a microscope for clearer understanding of the origin of life. Rarely, has an infancy ever been so exposed on canvas. Picasso segmented it into all its smallest parts; yet gathered together they make a child's whole life. He created twice: as father and as artist.

It was as though Picasso was an ever-searching camera, focusing on the foot in the mouth, the morsel of food as it was stuffed there too, the relaxed form as the child slept. He caught her as she was, as everyone's child is, every day. He dared to rearrange limbs to give an idea of the continuity of motion. The same picture caught a leg as it would be a moment later and as it was a moment before.

And he did not forget the delicious sweetness of childhood and its tyranny. He could see Paloma as she was: "She is a real monster. She is no baby any more, she is a woman," he said.

Crawling on the ground, devouring everything in sight, searching out, finding,

*Claude as Torero*
*1956    Ceramic tile      12×10"*

135

Paloma was reaching for her own world—*Paloma Playing* (Vallauris, February 2, 1950). Consider also the painting of a solemn Paloma (April 15, 1954), where the child investigates the formidable mystery of a tadpole's life cycle, and of her physical exuberance in Paloma jumping rope: one a canvas (1952-53), the other a statue, and both life size, almost mirroring each other, though they are quite differently made.

In the canvas, Paloma's eyes are concentrating on her feet: the rear foot is held high in the air as she soars, while the front foot just toes over the rope—the hands clutch the skiprope as tightly as a lifeline. Her torso is made up of angles and cubes, showing the body's movement. The whole is held together, framed by the loop of the rope itself. Paloma seems to hang in the air, yet she is grounded by the rope that whirls underfoot.

The sculpture is humorous, a parody of Paloma at play. It is made up of two old wicker wine baskets and a hemp rope. Her hair is corrugated paper cast in plaster, topped by a bow that looks like a small airplane ready to take off. On the child's feet is an actual pair of oversized discarded shoes. Here, too, the leaping child is anchored in the air by the rope underfoot—and suspended by it.

These twin documents of a child's uninhibited play have never been exhibited. The sculpture is complete, and there are two casts, but Picasso planned to paint and fire it, and for this reason it has never been shown. They both stand somewhere in a studio, still skipping rope long after Paloma has outgrown the game.

Paloma holding an orange and seated in a chair is in concept and effect like a detail from *Mother and Children with an Orange* (1951). And Paloma, alone, eating her lunch, spooning it up so greedily, concentrating on the dish, the spoon, is almost in the same way excerpted from *The Meal* (1953).

On December 25, 1953, a crouching Paloma hovers tenderly over her new toys in the garden, and the blossoms of the flowering shrub under which she plays look like decorations for a festive Christmas tree. The painting is a sunnier sectional study of the bitter *Figures in a Garden from a Window* (1953-54).

Picasso became an enthusiastic scholar of his children's baby talk. He listened

24.12.52.

*Paloma*
1952. Lithographie. 64 × 49 cm

solemnly as a tender paterfamilias to Claude's corruption of *"Cudyac"* for Cadillac. He wanted a ride. Paloma did not yet pervert the favorite onion pie, "la pissaladière," into "la-pisse-à-la-bière" as her brother had. Picasso managed, however, to make use of their uninhibited outpouring of scrambled meanings. In his play, *Four Little Girls,* he playfully uses the children's precocious stream of nonsense, shaped by invention, accident and inner violence.

They were always play-acting. Costumes were handy, so were masks—gifts from strange and distant lands—or they could be improvised. He also took them to the "theater of the sea" and taught them to swim. When Claude was not around, Picasso lay in the sand: swimming was for the children and he watched Paloma make a giant mural in the sand around him. In Paloma, almost more than in anything else, Picasso shows us the beauty in a child's everydayness. Here he records both as clinician and as doting father. In this dual commentary he has enriched our life with his unique appreciation of parenthood.

Picasso adores doves, *las palomas*. Yet he knows them very well: "They are greedy, quarrelsome birds," he said. But who are more greedy than children? How else can they grow?

He had sent his dove around the world as a symbol of his yearning for peace in April, 1949, and in his *Ronde des Enfants* (1952) he sent the child on that same errand. In Paloma, the child and the dove were combined, merged. The meaning was clear.

*Paloma*
*1951    Oil    10¾ × 8¾"*

*Paloma and Her Doll*
1952    Lithograph    28 × 21¾″

*Left*
*Paloma and Her Doll*
1952    Lithograph    28½ × 21¼″

*Right*
*Paloma Playing*
1950    Oil    49¼ × 40″

*Facing page*
*Paloma*
*1951    Oil    21½ × 18″*

*Left*
*Mother and Child*
*1951    Brush and ink    10 × 8″*
*Galerie Louise Leiris, Paris*

*Mother and Child*
*1951    Brush and ink    10 × 8″*
*Galerie Rosengart, Lucerne*

*Left*
*Mother and Child*
*1951    Brush and ink    10⅝ × 8½″*
*The Chapin and Mary Alexander*
*Riley Collection*
*Courtesy Worcester Art Museum*

Ceramic Dolls
1952

Paloma
1952   Oil   16×13″

*Paloma with Her Doll*
*1952    Oil    28½ × 23½"*

*Left*
*Paloma in Her Chair*
*1950    Oil    46 × 35"*

*Right*
*Paloma in Blue*
*1952    Oil    31½ × 25¾"*

VALLAURIS
1951
EXPOSITION

# "Come see the children"

In the family, the children are always around, a fact that emerges in the poems and paintings of Picasso's later years.

In *Poèmes et Lithographies* (1949), an edition of fifty numbered copies, published in 1954 by the Galerie Louise Leiris, he incorporates the children in his studio, whether indoors or outdoors.

> The I pulls his pipe from between his teeth—the II seated on the ground wrapped in ashes—a nude woman unfastening the flesh from her body two children playing in the wake of a brook running alongside the wall....
>
> The I puts his pipe back in the pocket of his mouth blows his nose scandalously and belches. The II lying on the ground snores sleeping—The children back on the grass drying their clothes in the shade....
>
> The 1400 francs given to the friend who came this morning bloom already ripe between the sheets—Come see the children.

At Vallauris, Picasso worked at fever pitch. Clay figures and bronzes crowded the sculpture studio; a garage became a storehouse for canvases; ceramics at the Madoura works were stamped with his name; Jean Arnera printed his posters as simply as children's drawings. Picasso even put his little Paloma on a poster for the annual exhibit of the Vallauris potters (1951).

Picasso's family was his love: his beautiful girl wife and their two children. He watched them eat; he watched the mother as she read or painted with the toddlers

*Vallauris Exposition*
*1951    Lithograph    25½×20"*

underfoot; he watched them all paint—and then he painted them. He made ceramic dolls with the hanging forelock of Claude or the chopped bangs of Paloma, both with the penetrating Picasso eyes. He called his children *les petits dessinateurs,* and so recorded them in a series of the same name, *The Little Sketchers* (1954), first alone, then with the hovering female figure guiding them. All the children draw: at first "to draw like Papa does"—as all children mime what their parents do—or like Mama, since Françoise Gilot was also a painter. But how much harder it is when one's father is the greatest painter alive.

How well do they draw? "Like children," is the careful answer.

When little Claude was brought to the studio at Vallauris, he left his chubby fingerprints on his father's work. The son watched his father paint, and chose three brushes to add his own individual touch. Paloma even formed funny faces in her ice cream with her spoon. She alone was allowed to take liberties with Picasso's themes and even to add her own. The children's art was respected. A Claude Picasso hangs beside a Pablo Picasso.

Picasso painted his love on canvas, and the love is there for all to see. It is no longer necessary to put in the words as he had in Cubist days: "Ma jolie," or "J'aime Eva."

Daniel-Henry Kahnweiler said: "His present painting exalts the beauty of his young wife and the grace of their small children."

And Picasso wrote:

> *To the trumpets of the bells which clung to her russet cheeks in the stickiness of the scribbles of soap bubbles of her shrieks melding the pink dress with red polka dots to the ardent white of the fragrant pastilles of her hair the sugar melted at the bottom of the cup and all the landscape enclosed inside the closed fists of the sun the fringes of the curtain covered with tacks decorating it decoratively with blue and green veronese oozing methodically hidden and carefully put under glass the music the fireworks and the perfumes of flying hands from some flowers set upright with their sticks stuck on the skin of the bread covered with ink agitating madly in the rules of the game and the ceremonies the caresses the menaces the*

*Three Profiles*
*1960*    *Lithograph*    24¼ × 19¼"

*blows all claws bared imitating timidly the orchestra of desires and the Orpheon*
*of disgusts agitating in the soup of their torn linen.*

Somehow, the young mother's eyes held a deep melancholy; the tenderness of parenthood is often missing from the canvases that portray her.

Things were not going well, and it showed in Picasso's work. If in the studio, studying the young models, or remembering them, he felt like an old painter, he painted that tragic situation, too: *The Old Artist in the Studio* (March 14, 1954). The span between the girl wife and the old artist grew perilously wide.

Soon, the children returned to Paris with their mother. Françoise Gilot was tired of sacrificing her gifted girlhood to his genius, of not knowing each day whether she was doormat or goddess.

His despair darkens *Figures in a Garden from a Window* (1953-54), where the children play solemnly yet contentedly with their new toys on Christmas Day, while he works sadly in the studio, his arm seemingly rended by the stripes of his Maillot. Now the children only came to see him on holidays and vacations. When they arrived, it was always a holiday. *Les Loisirs* (1956)—*The Amusements*—shows a family in a park or garden with small children, at leisure. Their joys are simple joys—bathing, dancing, walking, bicycling, all to flutes. His words and his canvases say: "Come see the children." He invites us in—and he shows them off, proudly.

*Claude and Paloma*
*1950    Oil    46×35"*

*Facing page*
*Figures in a Garden from a Window*
1953–54   Oil   59¼ × 38¼"
*Mr. and Mrs. David E. Bright,*
*Beverly Hills*

*The Old Artist in the Studio*
1954   Lithograph   13 × 20½"

*Overleaf*
*Claude and Paloma*
1950   Lithograph   20 × 30"

*Facing page*
*Mother and Children with an Orange*
1951    Oil    45¼ × 34¾"

*Claude and Paloma with Their Mother*
1951    *Ink and wash drawing*    9 × 12¼"
*Collection of Claude Gilot Picasso*

*The Family*
1953   Lithograph   15½ × 11″


*Right*
*Mother and Children*
1953   Etching   10¼ × 12¼″

*Mother and Children*
1953   Etching   10 × 12″

# 9　　*A Day in the Life of a Child*

Pablo Picasso has made a memorable record of the simple things that happen to a child every day.

A child's day may be made up of the same assorted bag of emotions as an adult's, but to the child the joy is greater, the pain hurts more, the hunger is stronger, and the sleep is deeper. Since, also, there is only a corner of understanding, suddenly brightly lighted up, and everything must open like a flower, petal after petal, or like a mystery unraveling, clue by clue, the process is often cubistic. It is, after all, the first time—and the imprint is forever.

Whether it is Claude or Paloma, or Paulo or Maya, or some other child who happened to catch his eye, or a child acting the part of an adult, the titles help to reveal the child's day: *Paloma Asleep* (1952), *First Steps* (1943), *The Meal* (1953), *The Playthings* (1950).

The child's day-to-day living provides the drama of Picasso's pictures. He adored those young years of wonderment, newness, rawness. Paulo's portraits, all in the classic tradition, stopped at five; sketches of Maya, sometimes freely done, more often realistically, stopped at eight. The two younger children had their babyhood mirrored and microscoped. There are a few pictures of an adolescent boy, and later there is the series of *The Woman and the Little Girls* (1960 and 1961) of Catherine Hutin, called Cathy, Jacqueline Roque's daughter, and his own Paloma, preadolescents, almost teenagers, no longer of chubby childhood and not yet formed. He managed to capture its uncertainty.

Mostly, however, the pictures are of little ones whose freshness shines through

*The Little Sketchers*
*1954　Lithograph　25 × 19¾"*

the distortions of Picasso's manner of the moment. How make something objective out of the subjective—the doll that is the small child's work, the human doll that is the adult's toy. The child eats and sleeps, and plays and loves, and discovers and takes his first halting step—a victory: "He walks!"

Tenderness and compassion pour out with the paint; then the father mocks his outbursts of sentiment.

These pictures are not only of his own children, and since with Picasso there is always more than meets the eye, another theme runs like a deep river beneath the simple surface of a child's day. Consider the children's pictures from the war years. Just as the tomato vine, potted and growing in a window, and turning to the sun, was a symbol of endurance and survival during those years, so Picasso frequently turned to childhood themes for renewal.

At Royan, where Picasso hurried once war was declared, in that first month of exile from Paris, he painted a *Seated Boy* (1939), defiant and wiggly, very reminiscent of Velázquez' *Boy of Vallecas,* who, because of his sharp and biting wit, was exiled from the court of Philip IV.

*First Steps* (1943) catches a child's early triumph, but is it not also a symbol of hope, at a time when all men were learning to walk, to fight back? What could be freer than those unstudied studies of the child and nursemaid in the park, études of September 1943? And what was more martial than the mere sketch of those marching feet across the sports page of the newspaper, when there was no drawing paper in Paris? That feast in *Child with Lobster* (1941), the child stark naked and abandoned to his pleasure on June 21, was a relief after the long cold winter when Picasso wrote the play, *Desire Caught by the Tail,* in which Onion was a character and the word "chilblains" a chant.

How low and oppressive the studio ceilings seem—it was August 24, and hot— to the crawler on the ground in *Child with Pigeons* (1943)! There, even the chair hems in the baby; once again the prevailing tones are blue, yet the pigeons are white. What was the war news then? On August 24, Tiger tanks were fighting fascists in Paris.

*Inez and Child*
1947    Pen    25 ¼ × 18 ½"
*Museum of Modern Art, New York*

Finally at war's end the small girl has her outing: *Little Girl Standing* (1945), in several variations on the same theme.

Now his attention was focused on the postwar infants: the baby daughter of the concierge with her extraordinarily long hair, and the newborn boy, son of Inez, his housekeeper at 7 rue des Grands-Augustins, of whom he made an annual birthday picture. In the long years of her service she had acquired a "collection."

With her son Girard in her lap, Inez posed for, or prompted, two lithographs, the year Claude was born. Girard is just a year older, and was frequently a companion of Claude's early years. Many photographs of the boys together as well as Picasso and the girls hang in Inez's living room below the studio.

The same year, *The Concierge's Daughter* (1947) at Number 7 was painted holding a doll, seated in a little chair, in sunny colors, cubistically patterned by the tears that course down her face in two dividing rivers. The sun also commanded the patterns on that post-cubist day, and the child sits in her chair in the same way that, long ago, a *Baby in Blue* (1901) sat in a chair. It was this cozy, small, self-contained world that Picasso responded to time and time again. It was peopled by the little ones he loved to watch, whose play he loved to share by his various modes of investigating their being.

*Studies of Woman and Child*
*1943   Drawing   8¾ × 5½"*
*Pages from a notebook*

*First Steps*
*1943    Oil    51¼ × 38¼″*
*Yale University Art Gallery*
*Gift of Stephen C. Clark*

*Study of Feet*
*1943    Oil on old newspaper    17 × 23½′*

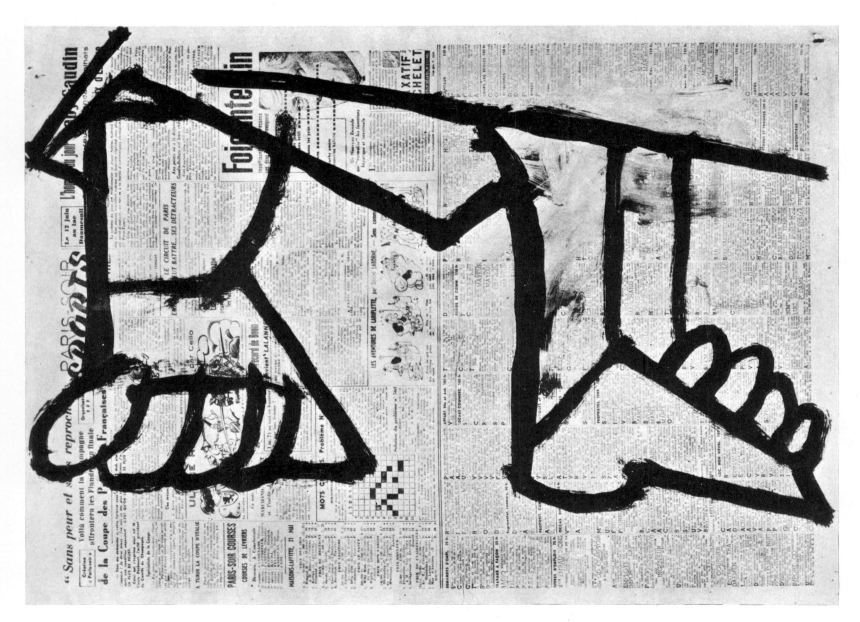

*Child and Lobster*
*1941    Oil    51 × 38"*

*Left*
*Child with Pigeons*
*1943    Oil    39⅜ × 31⅞"*

*Right*
*Seated Boy*
*1939    Oil    28½ × 23½"*
*Mr. and Mrs. Kirk Douglas,*
*Beverly Hills*

*The Meal*
1953   Oil   38×51″

*The Playthings*
*1950   Oil   46½ × 57"*

*Facing page*
*Little Girl Standing*
*1945    Oil    51 × 34½"*

*Paloma Asleep*
*1952    Oil    44⅞ × 57½"*
*Mrs. Bertram Smith, New York*

*To Amuse a Child*

"Let's pretend we are bullfighters," he would say to a child who was ill at ease in his presence. The game of growing is the play of a child's imagination: pretend to be mother, father, giant, a man from Mars. "You be a clown. I'll be Pierrot."

This childlike playfulness, inventiveness, creativity is a quality Picasso has never lost. A child's wonderment is constant because everything is for the first time. Picasso is a master of multiple aspects—that is, he is sophisticated and experienced, but with wonderment in reserve for the new view. He excels in seeing from still another point of view, at still another level in time and space. It was yesterday, it is today, it may be tomorrow; and he can transmit this insight so that we can feel what he feels.

"I am that child," he has said many times, in words and on canvas.

In 1938, in Mougins, Picasso made a series of pictures showing the universal child in man. When he used the "lazy ones" of Mougins as his models, he purposely sought out the most childish. *The Man with the Lollipop* (1938) was inspired by those village louts, mindless adults who were often seen sitting in the market place sucking over-sized lollipops. There is an ancient tradition in the Mediterranean world that the half-wit is in some way a magical character, a buffoon, contemptuously loved and mocked, and yet in essence a sacred creature; possessed by fairies, a fey one.

When Picasso admitted to an interviewer that the *Butterfly Hunter* (1938) was a self-portrait he was identifying with the clown, the Harlequin, the child in man. And this sense of play has served to lead him into every medium to nose out still another secret. It took him into new forms when he could have ridden his whole life through on the styles he left behind. He sees something new in something ordinary and twists

*Concierge's Daughter with Doll*
*1947    Oil    28½ × 36½"*
*Mr. and Mrs. Victor W. Ganz, New York*

it to his own use. He destroys one function and creates another. He is a contriver of glorious surprises.

Picasso has even used his children's discarded toys in shaping his sculpture: for instance, *Ape with Young* (1951). A toy motorcar ended up as the head of a baboon. You can still see it clearly as a motorcar, just as you can still identify the enormous beach ball that is the baboon's pregnant belly. And yet the total sculpture is very much baboon. A golf ball is the baby's head.

There are other magic transformations: the handlebars of an old bicycle, a piece of scooter, garbage-can lids and broom handles, turn into a bull, a bird and bathers. Everything is useful, for everything can be made into something else.

When Picasso decorates a casserole, he leaves the sides bare and turns it over to paint a face on the round bottom. Suddenly the casserole is a mask, and he lifts it to his face. He loves games because they combine the disciplined and the unexpected. If he makes a simple soup tureen as a gift, the recipient lifts the lid to find a picture inside. Once, he sent an ink drawing representing a platter to a bullfight promoter on the birth of a boy, and the platter was decorated with tiny dead bulls.

Picasso, who has dared everything, dared to sketch like a three-year-old and offered the comic mask as a catalogue cover for a show at the Galerie Louise Leiris in February, 1957, *"pour saluer Pablo Picasso."* If Paloma could try to paint like Picasso, he could paint like Paloma.

When Picasso is in the mood, he will dress up as a clown, as a sailor, a matador, a cowboy, or a woman. He will hide behind a shawl, a skirt, a ceramic pot, a plate, a plaster mask, and if nothing else is handy, he will tear up some paper to make a new mask or just add a nose: "Let's pretend!"

These masquerades have also ended up as decorations on his ceramics. Among the pictures that follow are some from the private collections of children, including Picasso's own grandson, Bernard. The clowns, sailors, and dwarfs—comedians of the human condition—were meant to amuse adults and children. More precisely, they were meant to amuse the child in all of us.

*Ronde des Enfants*
*1959    Lithograph    25 × 20"*
*Collection of Beatrice Glass, Paris*

*Left*
*Mother Ape and Child*
*1951    Bronze    21" high*

*King of the Clowns*
*1962    Lithograph    25 × 20"*
*Collection of Bernard Picasso*

*Clown*
1957    *Ceramic plate    17½" in diameter*
*The Saidenberg Gallery, New York*


*Left*
*The Old and the New Year*
1953    *Gouache, ink, crayon    19 × 15"*
*Musée de St-Denis, France*

*Facing page*
*Carnival*
*1961 Lithograph 25 × 20"*


*Père Noël*
*1959 Gouache 20 × 19½"*
*Musée de St-Denis, France*

*The Sailor*
1957    *Ceramic plate*
*Galerie Louise Leiris, Paris*


*Right*
*Père Noël*
1960    *Drawing and ink*
*Collection of Bernard Picasso*

pour Bernard,
son grand père
Picasso
le 18.12.
60.

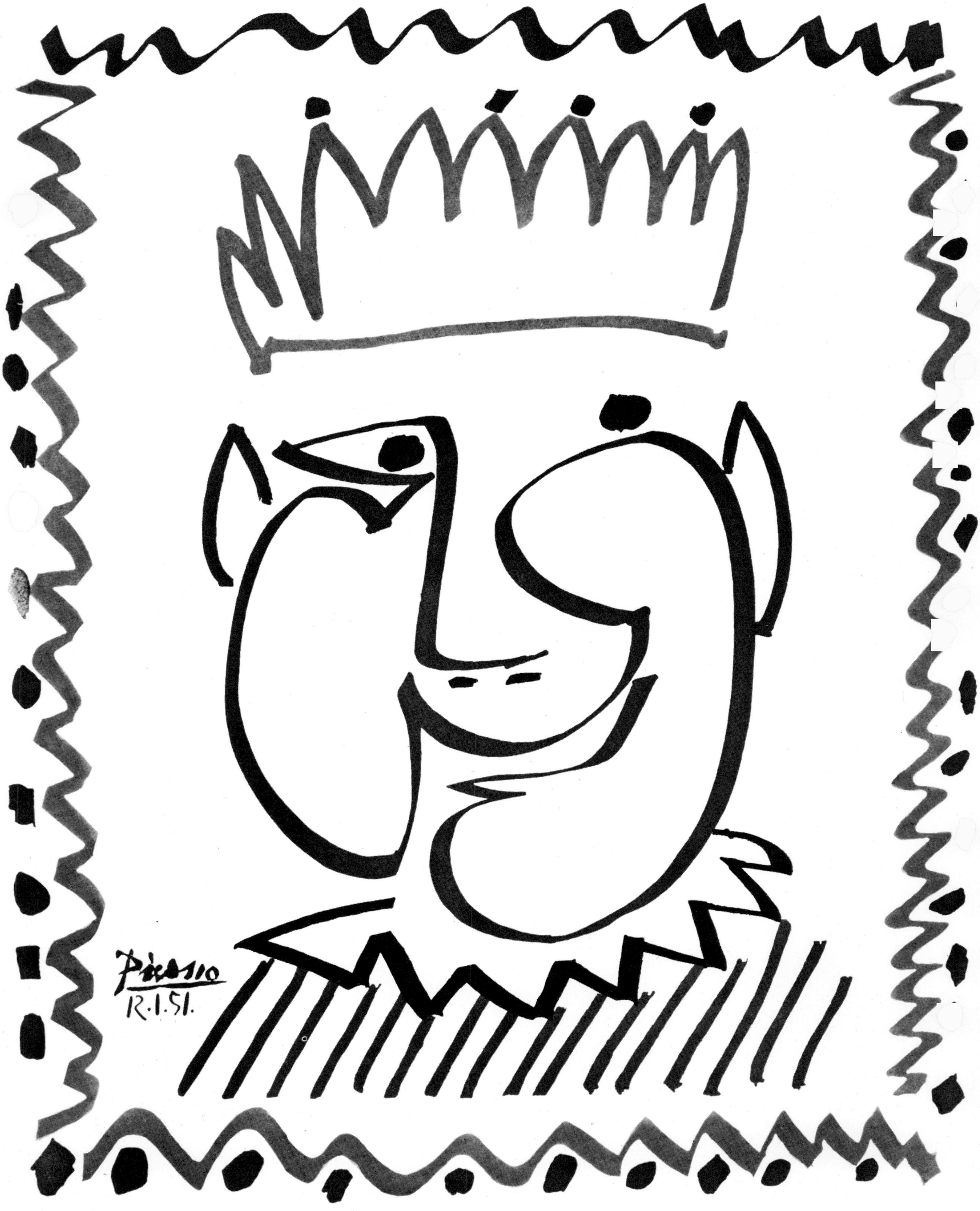
Picasso
R.1.51.

# II  *All the Dead Children*

Before Guernica, in his *Dream and Lie of Franco*, 1937, Picasso listed all the cries he heard:

> *Cries of children cries of women cries of birds cries of flowers cries of timbers and*
> *of stones cries of bricks cries of furniture of beds of chairs of curtains of pots of cats*
> *and of papers cries of odors which claw at one another cries of smoke pricking the*
> *shoulder of the cries which stew in the cauldron and of the rain of birds which*
> *inundates the sea which gnaws the bone and breaks its teeth biting the cotton wool*
> *which the sun mops up from the plate which the purse and the pocket hide in the*
> *print which the foot leaves in the rock....*

He made a series of etchings and wrote a poem in January, 1937, protesting the agony of his country. The etchings were to be like the beloved "aleluyas" of his boyhood, for mass distribution: two plates with eighteen picture postcards. The plates were so effective in their narrative continuity, expressing his rage at his country violated, that the engravings were left whole. Picasso had turned the humble cartoon strip into an art: the implacable sequence of ideas gathered into a sublime denunciation. These were the cries that he heard from his country—one long anguished sob of pain— and above all here was the despair of mothers with their children—no longer crying, but dead.

Simultaneously, in January, the Republican government had commissioned Picasso to paint a mural for the Spanish pavilion at the Paris International Exposition.

The attack on the Basque town of Guernica at 4:30 P.M. on April 26, 1937, be- came the "creative catalyst." On May 1, four days after the German Condor planes

*King of the Carnival*
*1951    Lithograph    21½ × 18"*
*Georges Tabaraux, Nice*

leveled the small capital, Picasso began his first sketches. Technically, *Guernica* is a canvas, but it is called a mural because of its vast dimensions: eleven feet six inches by twenty-five feet eight inches. Picasso made sixty studies for the *Guernica* and eight versions. In order to work on a painting of this size, he rented the high-ceilinged "Barrault loft" at 7 rue des Grands-Augustins.

The first sketches were of a dying horse, followed by ten studies of dead children. The lifeless child in the mother's arms equates the mortal wound of the dying horse— their open-mouthed agony is alike: the horse is symbol of all innocent suffering along with the mother and child. Guernica was a village of women and children, alone. The men were in the hills fighting.

Picasso's discoveries during Cubism, the pure line of his Neoclassic Period, and his long experiments with the human figure helped him through the complexities of the *Guernica,* where emotional impact was sought, and achieved, as violently as possible. Here, the distortions he had worked with, were used to show pain in both eyes, tears on both cheeks, on both sides of the face—the agonized collapse of broken bodies. As the war in Spain grew more and more apocalyptic, the dead child in the mural was moved to the left of the bull—the ultimate scream of all—a mother alive and her child dead.

Completed with extraordinary speed, a bare two months after the first drawings were begun, the *Guernica* was widely hailed as the greatest picture of the twentieth century—"no other picture portrays our age so completely."

Picasso, however, was not finished with the theme of the dead children. Their cries continued to haunt him all through that summer after the mural had been hung in its place of honor. He painted *Woman and Dead Child* (September 26, 1937), recalling that child on the left of the bull in the mural. It was not a painted study for the mural, not an afterthought, but an after-pain. It was a postscript to *Guernica,* foretelling what was to happen in all of Europe.

*Mother with Dead Child on Ladder*
*1937    Crayon and pencil    17⅛×9½"*
*The Museum of Modern Art, New York*
*On loan from the artist*

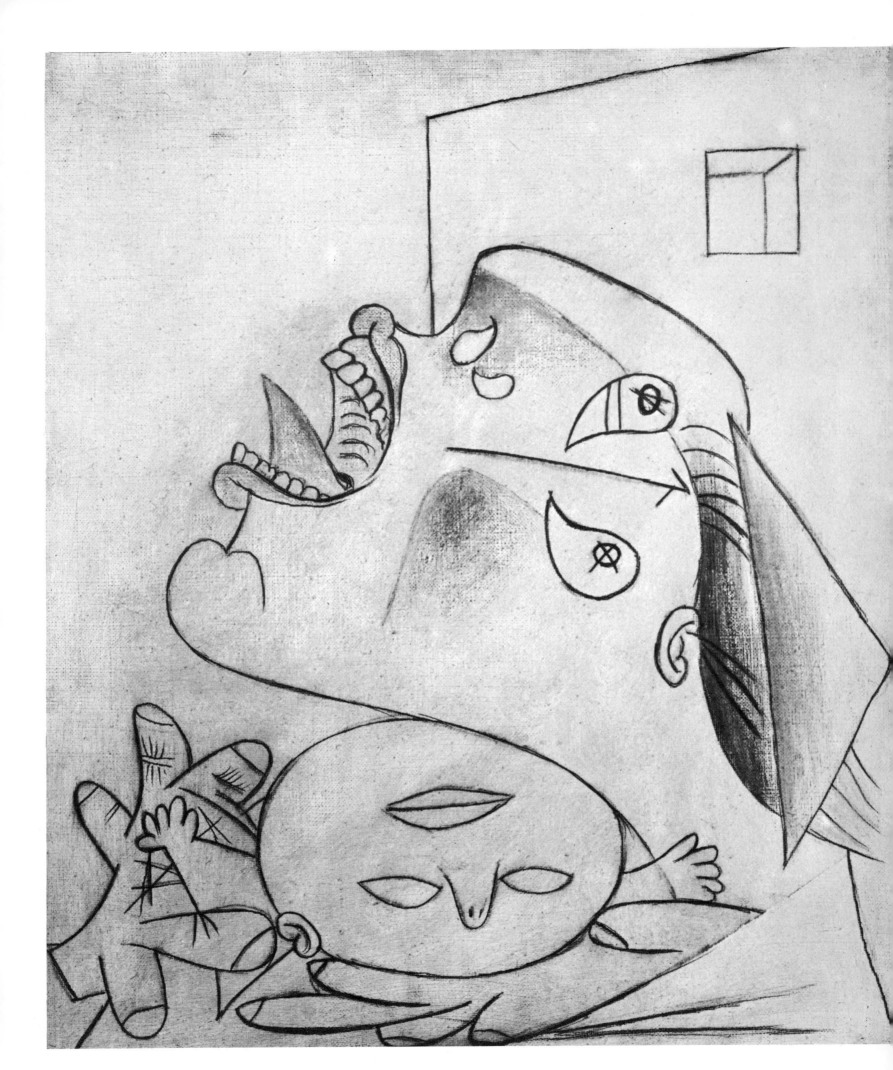

*Mother with Dead Child, 1937*
*Left      Pencil, crayon and oil      21⅝ × 18⅛"*
*Right     Pencil, crayon and gouache*
          *9¼ × 11½"*
*Below    Mixed media      9¼ × 11½"*
*The Museum of Modern Art, New York*
*On loan from the artist*

# Ronde des Enfants

"Can you find the hidden face?" the attendant asks as we enter the deconsecrated twelfth-century church at Vallauris, housing Picasso's mural *War and Peace* (1952). Since the mural is huge, War on one wall and Peace on the other, with a symbolic joining, finding the hidden face takes time. We must study all its parts, carefully.

First, participate in all the pleasures of a peaceful life: picnics, kiting, dancing, nursing babies. Don't forget the child harnessing Pegasus, or the owl roosting on the small boy's head, so obviously honoring his wisdom. But you cannot find the hidden face there, nor can you find it in the center piece which joins, unifies and hides nothing.

Turn then to the war section, and carefully search the war machine with all its hideous claptrap: warriors and weapons, blood and gore, and then behind a shield, beneath a dove's wings, discover the pale blue lines of a face. Now ask as a school child might of a devoted teacher: "Who is the hidden face?" The waiting attendant happily answers: "The hidden face is Peace."

Peace has the pure, serene features of Françoise Gilot. She and her children dominate the peace. The dove is there, amid the flood of war, ready to carry its peaceful message. The boy is there, plowing a peaceful world.

Picasso planned a mural as simple as primitive cave drawings, using the long hall of the building to that end. He meant the viewer to come upon each section as if in a prehistoric cave, lighted only by a torch to guide the spectator from one section to another. Searching for the hidden face also slows the spectator down so that he can study each separate theme.

The studies for *War and Peace* are bound in a book: *Etudes pour la Guerre et la Paix*.

*Mother with Dead Child*
*1937    Oil    51¼ × 76¾"*
*The Museum of Modern Art, New York*
*On loan from the artist*

These include the *ronde des enfants* that symbolize the peace, and are more moving than the mural itself. In the early days of May, 1952, they showed how a child's joy in living can become an artist's symbol.

Picasso was watching his own children dance, and he sketched his *rondes*. The *rondes* went on, around and around in peace, just as the children danced in life. Circling the Maypole, that totem of welcoming spring, around and around in increasing tempo, wild and exultant, heads back, faces up to the sky, hair and feet and skirts flying, one leg here, another there, a leg where it was a few moments ago, and the other in its place right now, and around once again with a final joyous leap for the biggest blossom on top of the tree—this was the dance of life.

Picasso's own joy dominates the theme—even the hidden face of peace, playfully put there for a child to find. His small children gave life to the *rondes*. Their mischief put wrens in fishbowls, and goldfish in bird cages, and sent up kites for the May breeze to blow—the reversed imagery of childhood and folk art. Here, too, is the reversed world of *art populaire,* the turnabout of accepted notions, the topsy-turvy pictures of fish fishing for men, of dogs at table and the sun and the moon on the grass.

Picasso found hope for the world in a child's simple dance. As a father he saw it, as an artist he captured its imagery, as a humanist he conceived it as a right to enjoy. In much the same way, men of good will looked at the realities of peace after war, and they too saw the peace as "the right of children to enjoy," and so proclaimed it.

These *rondes* are a lighthearted counterpart of the more solemn pronouncements of the United Nations: "Whereas mankind owes to the child the best it has to give...." With each right, they repeated: "The child has a right to enjoy ..."... *la ronde des enfants:* the "right to enjoy"... life ... *étude pour la paix.* The words had the sound of music.

*Ronde des Enfants*
*1952    Ink*
*Study for "The Peace"*

4 Mai 52.

*Studies for "The Peace"*
*1952    Ink*
*Pages from a notebook*

*Studies for "The Peace"*
1952    *Ink*
*Page from a notebook*

*Right*
*Boy and Owl*
*Detail from "The Peace"*

*Overleaf*
*Detail from "The Peace"*

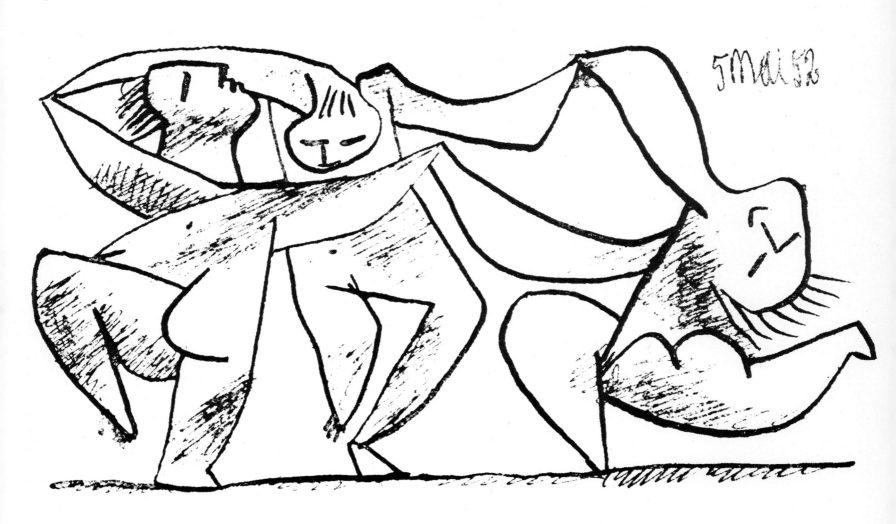

# 13                    *Las Meninas*

There is a key to the riddle of *Las Meninas*—The Maids of Honor. It lies buried in
the archives of the Prado in the original name Velázquez gave to the painting before
the little Spanish princess—the Infanta—and her maids of honor stole the title for
themselves. Babies and pigeons, *Bambini e colombe,* the Italians called Picasso's conversations with Velázquez' *Las Meninas.* They were close to turning the key that
would unlock the riddle.

In order to use that key, we must go back, like Picasso, to the original Velázquez
painting, and we must remember that he was only a boy of fourteen when he had his
first conversation with Velázquez at the Prado, in Madrid. There *Las Meninas* is the
only painting in a room, even though it is not alone.

Velázquez, too, had preferred his mother's name rather than his father's in signing
his paintings. Among the first Spaniards to paint the humbler aspects of life, with
models drawn from all sorts and conditions of mankind, Velázquez became court
painter in his early twenties. In late life he could play ... even with the royal family.
In *Las Meninas,* painted when he was fifty-five years old, he amused himself by
putting King Philip IV and his Queen Mariana of Austria out of their own picture
and the painter into it. By this act of *lèse-majesté*—this playful affront to his sovereigns,
Velázquez achieved a poetic synthesis of his technical repertoire and created one of
the supreme pictorial masterpieces of all time.

*Las Meninas* is a picture within a picture, a world within a world, and so begins
a cycle of reflections.

Velázquez stands behind an easel, painting the unseen king and queen. Even the

*Study for "The Peace"*
*1952   Ink*
*Page from a notebook*

canvas representing them is unseen: its back is to the spectator, except as it is reflected in a mirror at the rear of the room. The five-year-old Infanta Margarita captures the center of the stage as she walks in with her maids of honor, her dwarfs, her mastiff, and the ladies-in-waiting to look at her parents' portrait. Yet no one in the painting is looking at the canvas: they are all looking out—toward the spectator. The king and queen, then, must be standing with the spectator. We know they are there, because the *aposentador mayor,* the official of the King's household who travels before the royal family to prepare for their reception, is just walking out the door.

Today, at the Prado, the full-size painting faces an equally large mirror, emphasizing Velázquez' play with reflections: the reflection of the royal personages in the mirror within the painting; the reflection of the painting itself, as if painted by another artist outside the canvas, rather than by the painter in the painting. Finally, the mirror allows those in the canvas to become spectators along with the king and queen. The real subject then seems to be not in the picture at all; the real subject is the eternal spectator.

It became a game for Pablo Picasso to make his own "reflections on reflections on reflections." In four months in the autumn of 1957 he painted fifty-eight canvases—his conversations with Velázquez, in a third-floor studio prepared especially for this purpose: the dovecot at La Californie.

"For the sake of Velázquez, because of Velázquez, Picasso resolved to carry on his dialogue with the master of Seville in a place apart: alone, all outside noises excluded, he communed with the spirit of Philip IV's court painter and studied the maids of honor…" explained Jaime Sabartès, friend of Picasso's youth, who once had playfully asked to be sketched as a courtier to another Spanish King, Philip II, and found that Picasso had as playfully obliged him (1939).

Alone, with his ground-hugging dog and his high-flying pigeons, Picasso conversed with Velázquez. He displaced Velázquez in the painting and put himself behind the easel. He changed vertical lines to horizontal ones in the composition, and set about putting his symbols, his own games, within Velázquez' riddle. He played house in the great master's work, and he painted his own dachshund Lump where the king's aristocratic hound had sat. Gradually he welcomed his own family into his own variations on the theme.

The maids of honor were dissected, dismembered, destroyed, and reborn, along with the golden infanta, in studies, small and large, in blues, grays, and yellows, and in monochrome. Picasso parodied both Velázquez and himself, clowning outrageously. He played practical jokes on Velázquez and himself.

When it seemed to him that the raised hand of the buffoon looked more like a boy playing the piano, Picasso painted in a piano and let the boy play to his heart's content, *The Piano* (1957), as he had once joyfully added to his friend's bare room all the necessities of life and spirit with his gift—decorations on the wall.

To be symbolically Picasso's own variations, there had to be pigeons. He opened the windows facing the sea and painted the Côte d'Azur: the giant palms and the deep blue sea. Framed in the window were the roosting pigeons, whose home was the studio. They had hatched there in the coops that Picasso himself had built. They had been fed and tended with his own hands. "They think I am their mother," he said. Perhaps he was remembering the picture his father had painted with "hundreds, no thousands and millions of pigeons in a coop." He raised these *palomas* from a single pair, gifts from a Spanish friend. He let them fly free, as his father had. In a year there were forty, and they flew in and out of his rooms, alighting indiscriminately on canvases and beds, frames of pictures on the walls, bureaus and chairs; roosting; moulting; multiplying; their droppings and feathers a part of the studio, as Hélène Parmelin has vividly described.

He made nine paintings of the sea and the pigeons. In 1961, the Commissariat Général au Tourisme had a lithograph made of one by Henri Deschamps and printed by Mourlot as a poster to attract tourists to the Côte d'Azur.

Only Jacqueline Roque was allowed to climb to the top floor and watch Picasso as he worked. There he painted a queenly portrait of her on December 3, 1957, to join the other canvases of the maids of honor. The children came down for the holidays, and the last painting was finished on the last day of the year: a curtsying little girl, adorable: "Come, papa, join us," she beckons. This small dark-haired child is no longer the Velázquez Infanta—she is Picasso's very own. He had exhausted the theme.

Picasso's variations on the theme have given meaning to the original name of the Velázquez painting. The maids of honor, surrounding the golden-haired Infanta, herself honoring the painter, gave the picture its popular title, but the first name Velázquez chose for his great composition was simply *La Familia,* the family of Philip IV. The king and queen, then, standing outside their own picture, were in fact the creators of *La Familia.* It was painted as though the king was the artist. In the same way, Picasso made Velázquez' *La Familia* his own family.

"Yo el rey," he had written on the brow of his self-portrait at eighteen years, before his first trip to Paris. At almost eighty, he replaced the king with his own reflection in the mirror at the back of the room.

But wait ... whose face is in the mirror that reflects the spectator-creator? Who stands outside Picasso's own *Las Meninas?* A dead-white face with upturned grin, merrily mocks all from the mirror at the back of the room. It is the Harlequin— Picasso's symbol. It is this symbol which links Picasso the novice and Picasso the master.

The whole series of Picasso's *Las Meninas* was given to the Barcelona Museo de Arte Moderno. It is now proudly placed along with Sabartès' personal collection of drawings in a beautiful seven-hundred-year-old castle, the Palacio Aguilar in the Gothic quarter of the old Catalan capital, near Barcelona Cathedral, where Picasso grew up. All the city-owned works by Picasso are now housed here in the Picasso Museum, Calle de Moncada, 15. Every detail of its renovation—the placing of pictures, the selection of furniture, even the colors on the wall—was personally attended to by Jaime Sabartès as perhaps his last service to his old friend. Located in Franco's Spain, in Barcelona, that window facing France, this particular Picasso museum delayed its official opening, and then was quietly declared officially open.

*Las Meninas by Velázquez*
*The Prado, Madrid*

*The Maids of Honor, after Velázquez*
*1957    Oil    76⅓ × 102⅓"*

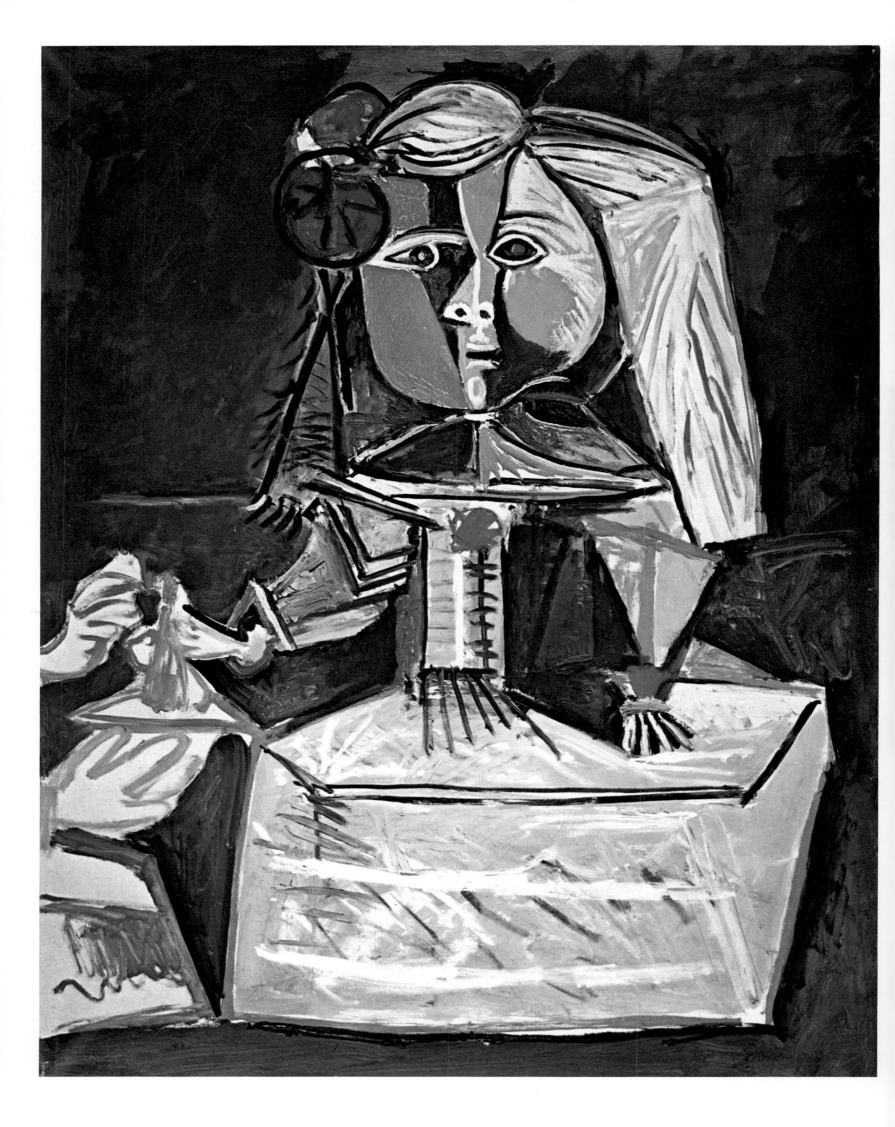

*The Infanta*
1957    Oil    18 × 14½"

*Left*
*The Infanta*
1957    Oil    31¾ × 36"

*Right*
*The Maids of Honor*
1957    Oil    51¼ × 37¾"

*The Infanta*
1957     *Oil*     13×9½"

*Left*
*The Infanta*
1957     *Oil*     13×9½"

*Right*
*The Pigeons*
1957     *Oil*     39⅓×31½"

## 14  *Grand-père Picasso*

The only pictures Picasso ever made of a grandchild were of Bernard, son of Paul. They were made on a single day, on November 9, 1959, in a fast few moments, as a gift for his beloved Bernard, Picasso's third grandchild. The baby was newborn, only a few days old, almost a birthday gift for the grand-père himself.

Before I left Paris, I went to see Paul Picasso in his apartment in the rue du Vieux-Colombier on the Left Bank. He and his wife Christine greeted me in English which they spoke fluently. On the center table in their living room I showed them my *maquette* or dummy, the form the book was to take. Small Bernard was riding around the room on his bicycle as we thumbed through the pages. He stopped and came over; he wanted to see the pictures too. I picked him up and sat him in my lap and showed the book the way I had dreamed all children could enjoy Picasso's accolade to childhood—in the arms of an adult.

Christine looked over my left shoulder; Paul was on my right; Bernard sat very still as we turned the pages.

When we came to the chapter titled "Grand-père Picasso," there were a few pictures of a Picasso grandchild I had found in a magazine. I turned to Paul and said: "I am looking all over for the originals and cannot find them. Do you know where they are?"

"But they are mine," Paul answered. "They are right here...."

Christine ran into the dining room and took them out of a chest. Bernard went back to his bicycle as we followed her. The collection was in a wrapper, the outer cover somewhat frayed, but they were there, a sequence of living moments.

*The Piano*
*1957   Oil    51¼ × 37¾"*

*Bernard Picasso with His Mother, Christine*

10.11.59.

They were of an infant. The line began delicately, lightly as an infant's sleep; then became bolder, as strong and penetrating as a baby's hunger cry. Here was a home cinema of a child awakening from sleep: a sudden spasm of hunger, a pain that distorts the baby face and makes it shriek its needs, a smile that speaks of comforting hands reaching out to hold him. The camera shifts its focus, takes the drama from the child and turns it on the mother.

I was greedy. "Do you have others?" I asked.

"No," Paul answered.

"Are there others of your other children—Marina and Pablo?"

"No," Paul repeated, looking quickly at Christine. "There are no others. Of no other grandchildren, only these."

Christine led us into Bernard's nursery. She wanted to show me the baby's per-

sonal Picasso collection, but Paul interrupted her. He had something special in mind.

He took an object from the shelf. "See, what he made for Bernard," Paul said, "a hobbyhorse."

He held out the welded horse, painted white with an elongated head; the back of the head was parallel to the neck, and it had long cut-out slits for eyes and a wisp of a tail. It was set on two triangles for legs with large brass casters as feet. Bernard left the bicycle to glide on his hobbyhorse as we talked.

"May I photograph it?" I asked.

"Of course. Photograph it with Bernard sitting on it," Paul laughed.

After watching Bernard for a moment, Paul changed his mind. "I think I would rather keep this private, just for Bernard," he said.

Instead he brought out a little red *torero* costume with shining gold braid—still in

*Bernard Picasso*
*with His Mother, Christine*

219

its box, resting regally on white tissue paper. "I bought this when I went to the bull-fights," he explained, since he had just returned from a visit to Arles with his father to see the season's performers from Spain.

Bernard reached up to touch the little red suit. He would have liked to put it on then and there, but it was left in the box for a special occasion. It was to be a surprise – to be worn at Bernard's first bullfight. Like all the Picasso children, he must learn about bullfighting while he is young. When then?—as his grandfather believes. Or perhaps he would wear it for grand-père on his birthday?

Christine pointed out Bernard's private gallery hanging over his crib.

He has his own Père Noël (1960), dedicated to him by his grandfather: *"Pour mon petit Bernard,"* and the *King of the Clowns* (1962), also autographed specially for him. He also had the picture of a child removing a Père Noël mask—*The Old and the New Year* (1953)—and another of the *King of the Carnival* (1951), made for the city of Nice, the face composed of two doves.

*"Shalom,"* I said to Yona, their dog, in recognition of her Hebrew name. Christine is half Israeli and had named her. It was an amusing name, for she was so unlike a pigeon—large and shaggy and quite heavy. I knew this from experience; she had jumped on me in greeting and did so now in farewell.

*"Shalom,"* Christine answered, her dark eyes bright and deep.

*Right and overleaf*
*Bernard Picasso, 1959*

9. 11. 59.

pour Bernard

9.11.59.

When Picasso began to play with Manet's sophisticated *Déjeuner sur l'herbe,* a baby and his world crept into his studies. Manet's masterpiece, which shocked the Victorians and was refused exhibition, had nothing so simple as a playing infant.

Picasso's studies, begun at Vauvenargues, were worked on at La Californie and finished at Mougins. He communed with Manet on all levels but he added his own fillip, the study of a child, because it was there—an infant on the grass..

On June 6, 1961, Picasso made eleven sketches of two female bathers and a baby. One woman slept in the sun and the other dried her feet, eventually putting on her sandals.

Meanwhile the child at their feet had conquered a whole world; he had explored and changed his environment, though he did not even crawl away. In sequence, the drawings are almost animated frames for a cartoon strip, each one drawn as though it were just a moment later in time. Five drawings show the crawling lump of childhood playing with a sailboat in a tub, with a discarded toy horse beside him. Two show the baby pulling a toy train; then he finds a turtle, and his discovery is so tremendous that he raises himself on his arms and stares at the turtle, which in turn has conveniently put its head out to look at him.

During all this time one woman continues to tie her shoe, while the other sleeps.

Suddenly a pigeon flies in front of the baby and stays there. Both baby and pigeon turn to the women, hoping for some sign of appreciation of this miracle, but the faces of the women do not change. Only the baby changes. Faceless and formless though the infant is, he shows surprise, interest and worry as he becomes acquainted

*Left and overleaf*
*The Bathers*
*1961*    12½ × 19½"
*From Picasso's "Les Déjeuners"*

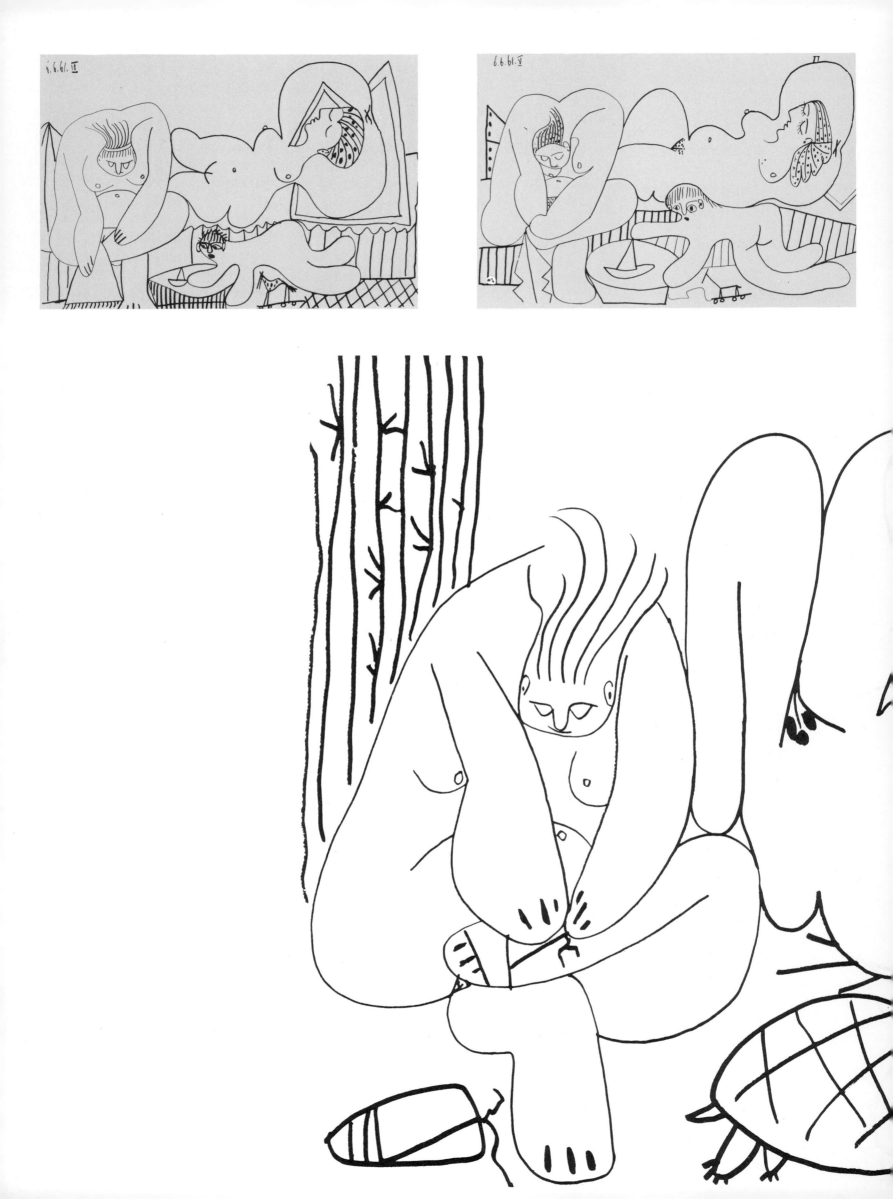

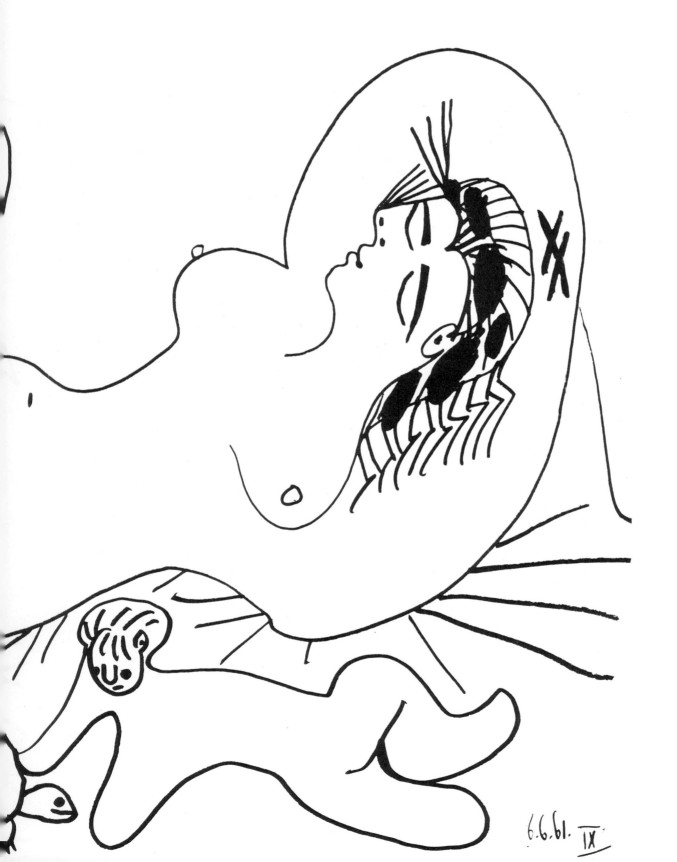

with the turtle, pleased and proud to know it. When the bird rests beside him, even from the back of his head and the position of his body one sees the child's intensity and his hope that the women too may see what he sees, may respond to this adventure.

Two months later, after Picasso moved to Notre-Dame-de-Vie, he again drew the baby with *The Bathers* (1961), still at the women's feet. The playthings in the foreground are a new basket and a hat. Life continues.

# 16                    *Our Lady of Life*

The roads approaching Picasso's home near Mougins are plastered with signs reading: Notre-Dame-de-Vie, like friendly directions for reaching his new villa. But the signs are misleading: they are meant for the twelfth-century church near by.

Picasso bought *le domaine de Notre-Dame-de-Vie* in the summer of 1961. It is secluded behind high iron gates with an electric calling system—to ensure privacy. When a high-rise, multiple dwelling, mushroomed out of the valley and blotted out his view, Picasso finally left the rue de Costabelle, and the villa La Californie, in Cannes, and moved to Notre-Dame-de-Vie at Mougins. He left, even though there he had been fondly called "le roi de Californie."

This is home now much more than the château of Vauvenargues near Aix-en-Provence, which he had bought in 1958. Picasso was moved to own the other side of Mont Sainte-Victoire, the mountain Cézanne had painted. It amused him even more to find himself a successor of the eighteenth-century moralist, the Marquis de Vauvenargues. The majestic surroundings stimulated the Spain within, and at Vauvenargues themes, colors, and moods of his native country came somberly into his canvases.

Even the *lazarillos,* the little street arabs of Murillo, seemed to walk through the woods towards Vauvenargues from Spain, and in remembering them, he painted the all-seeing *"Bobo," after Murillo* (1959), homage to the man who had painted so many of these wise and knowing homeless boys.

In *The Dining Room* (1959), the Spanish influence accents his domesticity. The heavy commode, dark and brooding, overshadows the seated child and the leggy Dalmatian. The bleak harshness of the mountains gave Picasso the solitude he needed

*The Bathers*
*1961*    12½ × 19½"
*From Picasso's "Les Déjeuners"*                                        **229**

for work, yet he did not choose this place as a permanent residence. Instead, he turned again to Mougins, where he had lived before, and bought a hillside opposite the medieval mountain village commanding a view of the countryside and sea—*le domaine de Notre-Dame-de-Vie*. "Our Lady of Life" was an appropriate home for a man who still had much to do. Atop his aerie, at the end of a winding driveway half a kilometer long, he works ... works ... works....

Here, Jacqueline Roque Picasso reigns securely as his new wife. The children come home on holidays, his and hers: Cathy, from boarding shool in Cannes, and Paloma from Paris. Cathy's parents were divorced in French West Africa long ago when she was an infant. She calls Picasso "Pablito"; he is a tender father to her, also. The girls are but a year apart. Their circled and unformed faces, when they were ten and eleven years old, inspired a series of four canvases, *The Woman and the Little Girls* (1960-61).

Sometimes his work and his domestic life are interrupted by reports from the various parts of his kingdom: his subjects wait long for appointments. One of the Mourlots comes down to show progress on a new book of lithographs; a man to have an old painting authenticated; Kahnweiler or Louise Leiris to ask about an exhibition or to bring news from the galleries; Jean Arnera of Vallauris to show him proofs of the new linoleum blocks; the Ramiés of the Madoura potteries to talk of ceramics; Catalan friends to ask for help in another disaster—a flood in October 1962.

Only a few days after their plea, Picasso sent a painting, *Jacqueline with Shawl and Dog* (1959), from the Vauvenargues Period. Exhibited for the first time that spring at the Galerie Louise Leiris, it had been marked: "Not for sale." He was saving it for the Family Gallery. But now, it left Nice by air for Barcelona to help the Catalans.

The days when there are no interruptions are his best, for there are even the rocks to collect and decorate. His imagination, like curiosity itself, goes on being insatiable. Paul Eluard in his poem *"à Pablo Picasso"* called him "that mirror of flesh in which a child is pearled." Adapting Picasso's remarks of long ago on his father's pigeons, we can say that he remains more curious than a hundred ... no a thousand ... million children.

*The Woman and the Little Girls*
*1960    Oil    51 × 38"*

*Left*
*The Woman and the Little Girl*
*1960    Oil    63½ × 51"*

*The Woman and the Little Girl*
*1961    Oil    63½ × 51"*

*The Woman and the Little Girls*
*1961    Oil    57½ × 44¾″*

*The Dining Room*
*1959    Oil    76½ × 110″*

# Acknowledgments

Very special thanks is due the Galerie Louise Leiris: Daniel-Henry Kahnweiler, Mme Louise Leiris, and Maurice Jardot for all their help with pictures, and for permission to use extracts from *Poèmes et Lithographies,* published by the Galerie Louise Leiris, Paris, 1954.

For help with the translations, I wish to thank my beloved friends: Noémi Perelman Mattis, Maryse Sudour Burns, and express my appreciation to Henriette d'Arlin for her translation of the Kahnweiler Foreword and Picasso's poems.

Thanks is also due Louis Untermeyer for allowing me to use a verse from his translation of Heinrich Heine's "Lyrical Intermezzo."

I wish to thank Paul Steiner and Chanticleer Press: Milton Rugoff, editor; Miss Ann Guilfoyle, editorial associate, and Ulrich Ruchti, director of design.

I am also grateful to M. Gilliard of SPADEM, Paris, and Horace Marston of French Reproduction Rights, New York.

I am grateful to the following for permission to reproduce material from published sources: Cahier d'Art, Paris; Pierre Cailler, Geneva; *Verve,* Revue Artistique, Paris; André Sauret, Editions du Livre, Monte Carlo; Joseph Foster, *Picasso's Posters,* Crown Publishers, New York; *Etudes pour la Guerre et la Paix, Les Déjeuners, Les Ménines,* Editions Cercle d'Art, Paris.

For permission to reproduce pictures in their collections, I am indebted to the following: The Thannhauser Foundation, New York; Galerie Charpentier, Paris; Lionel Prejger, Knoedler's, Paris; M. and Mme Frédéric Schnerb, Paris; Dr. and Mrs. Andrew M. Linz, New York; Union Centrale des Arts Décoratifs, Ville de Grenoble, France; The City Art Museum of St. Louis; The Maurice Wertheim Collection, Fogg Museum, Harvard University; Lady Aberconway, London; Courtauld Institute, London; Musée des Beaux-Arts, Liège; Goya Museum, Castres, France; The Abrams Family Collection,

*"Bobo," after Murillo*
*1959    Oil    36×28¾"*

237

New York; Chester Dale Collection, National Gallery of Art, Washington, D.C.; Violette de Mazia, Barnes Museum, Merion, Pa.; Galerie Bernheim, Paris; Mr. and Mrs. William Goetz, Los Angeles, Calif.; Dial Collection of the Worcester Art Museum, Worcester, Mass.; Hermitage, Leningrad; Mr. and Mrs. Harold Crang, Toronto; Mr. and Mrs. Kirk Douglas, Beverly Hills, Calif.; Mr. and Mrs. David E. Bright, Beverly Hills, Calif.; The Albright-Knox Art Gallery, Buffalo, N.Y.; Baltimore Museum of Art; Mr. and Mrs. Julian C. Eisenstein, Washington, D.C.; Kunstmuseum, Gothenburg, Sweden; Meta and Paul J. Sachs Collection, Fogg Museum, Harvard University; Kunstmuseum, Stuttgart, Germany; The Hon. and Mrs. William A. Burden, New York; The Tate Gallery, London; William S. Paley, New York; Kunstmuseum of Basel, Switzerland; Cleveland Museum of Art, Cleveland, Ohio; The Hon. and Mrs. W. Averell Harriman, New York; Mr. and Mrs. Aaron Ginsburg, New York; Galerie Rosengart, Lucerne, Switzerland; Chapin and Mary Alexander Riley and Worcester Art Museum, Mass.; Picasso Arts, Inc., New York; Mrs. Bertram Smith, New York; Mr. and Mrs. Lawrence Saidenberg, New York; The Saidenberg Gallery, New York; Samuel M. Kootz, Samuel M. Kootz Gallery, Inc., New York; Alex Maguy Gallery, Paris; Beatrice Glass, Paris; Paul Picasso, Paris; Bernard Picasso, Paris; Musée de St-Denis, France; Yale University Art Gallery, gift of Stephen C. Clark; Mr. and Mrs. Victor W. Ganz, New York; Georges Tabaraux, Nice; Mme Helena Rubinstein, New York; Robert Sincerbeaux of Sincerbeaux and Sincerbeaux, New York, executors of the Eva Gebhard Foundation, The Baroness Gourgaud, New York and Paris; Musée des Arts Décoratifs, Paris; The Art Institute of Chicago, gift of Mary and Leigh Block Charitable Fund, Inc.; Mr. and Mrs. Edwin E. Hokin, Maymar Corporation; Mr. and Mrs. Chauncey McCormick; Mrs. Maurice L. Rothschild, and the Ada Turnbull Hertle Fund.

I also wish to thank the following for assisting or supplying me with photographs: Galerie Louise Leiris, Paris; Musée des Arts Décoratifs, Paris; Museum of Modern Art, New York; Giraudon, Paris; Savage Studios of St. Louis; Sy Kattelson, Woodstock, N.Y.; The Buckinghams, Thornwood, N.Y.; The Art Gallery of Toronto, Canada; Fine Arts Engravings Studio, London; René Revillon, Draeger Frères, Paris; *Verve,* Revue Artistique, Paris; Fernand Hazan, Paris; McCullagh Studio, Toronto, Canada; André Held, Lausanne, Switzerland; Dr. Alfred M. Frankfurter and *Art News,* New York; Studio Vallois, Paris; Sandak, New York; Conzett and Huber, Zurich.

# List of Reproductions by Chapters

239

*Designed by Ulrich Ruchti*